The Cinema of ALAIN RESNAIS

In the same
**INTERNATIONAL
FILM GUIDE SERIES**
edited by Peter Cowie

THE
CINEMA
OF
ALAIN RESNAIS

by

ROY ARMES

*This is what makes the cinema an
art: it creates a reality with
forms. It is in its form that
we must look for its true content.*
ALAIN ROBBE-GRILLET

A. ZWEMMER LIMITED, LONDON
A. S. BARNES & CO., NEW YORK

Acknowledgements

IN THE compilation of this book I have incurred a deep debt of gratitude to the innumerable journalists and film critics who have provoked and recorded Alain Resnais's comments on his art. Their names are to be found in the bibliography, to which the numbers after each quotation in the text refer.

I am also grateful to the British Film Institute, Contemporary Films, Peter Cowie, Gala Film Distributors, Sebricon Productions, L'Avant-Scène, Allen Eyles, and United Artists Corporation for the provision of stills.

Above all, my thanks go to Alain Resnais himself for taking time off to talk to me about his work and for providing some of the illustrations.

COVER STILLS

Front: Alain Resnais, and Yves Montand and Ingrid Thulin in LA GUERRE EST FINIE.
Back: Top, L'ANNÉE DERNIÈRE À MARIENBAD; centre, MURIEL; below, HIROSHIMA MON AMOUR.

FIRST PUBLISHED 1968

Copyright © 1968 by Roy Armes
Library of Congress Catalog Card No.: 68-15195
This edition prepared by The Tantivy Press
in association with A. Zwemmer Limited
and A. S. Barnes & Co. Inc.

Printed in Holland by
Drukkerijen vh Ellerman Harms nv, Amsterdam

Contents

For Caroline, Philip and Helen,
who wanted a green book.

1. The Director's Role

> *. . . L'autre danger serait de devenir une sorte de statue, de s'imaginer qu'on est l'auteur pour lequel les gens vous prennent.* ALAIN RESNAIS

A NY STUDY of Alain Resnais's work must begin with a consideration of the question of the authorship of his films, if only because of his own often repeated disclaimer: "Do I consider myself to be the author of my films? No; but above all I consider that this does not interest me."[5] In the sense in which the term author *(auteur)* has come to be used in French film criticism — to denote a complete creator as opposed to a 'mere' director — it is clear that it cannot meaningfully be applied to Resnais. He is, in terms of this distinction, a director *(metteur en scène)* and recognises himself as such: "I consider myself a *metteur en scène* in the precise meaning of the term."[4] In almost twenty years of professional film-making he has never written a single line of script, a word of dialogue, nor even put in, Jorge Semprun tells us[60] of *La Guerre est finie*, so much as a comma. Resnais's work lacks too the obsessional quality of a true 'author' — he does not constantly remake the same film, nor reiterate time and time again certain central propositions that dominate his view of life. Although there is a remarkable thematic as well as stylistic unity in Resnais's work, the themes, problems, ideas are each time handled from a fresh angle and any attempt at generalisation is extremely hazardous. To take a simple example: it is true to say that all Resnais's feature film scenarists reject the traditional pattern of film construction

9

and that all are fascinated by the question of time, but what is important is that the stylistic answer each gives to the structural problem and the particular facet of time dealt with in each film are distinctive and individual. The essence of *L'Année Dernière à Marienbad* lies in the way it is different from *Hiroshima mon Amour* or *Muriel* and any attempt to interpret one film in terms of another (to consider, for instance, *Marienbad* as a study of memory because of the other two films) is fraught with pitfalls.

Another aspect of this refusal of 'authorship' is shown by Resnais's remarkably detached attitude to his chosen medium. He lacks, if we are to believe his own words, any driving compulsion to express a personal vision on celluloid and, questioned on this point in 1964, he said: "I do not intend to dedicate my whole life to the cinema: I'm quite willing to sacrifice fifty per cent of my existence to it, but not more than that"[30]. Asked what film-making represents for him he replied that first of all it is a means of existence (not, one notes, of expression). His progress from film to film is the result of external pressures, not an inner compulsion — this he has made clear and it is important to approach his work in this light. In the revealing interview published in 1960 he said: "When I am shooting it is impossible for me — as for anyone else — to stand outside. But when finished I do not try to rush into another film, as someone with urgent messages to deliver would no doubt do. Every time it is material necessity that forces me to accept a certain proposition. I have always made commissioned films and I've never wanted to make the film which was proposed to me. I prefer working as film editor, it is less absorbing from every point of view"[5]. There is certainly an excessive degree of modesty here, as in many of Resnais's statements about his role in the cinema, but it does define his approach.

Alain Resnais, then, is a *metteur en scène*, no more, no less, and to talk of 'the films of Alain Resnais' is not to deny that important contributions have been made to these works by other people. Indeed his approach to the cinema is one that demands creative contributions from all the people concerned in the film. The director is not the sole creative force and the notion of collaboration is one of the bases of Resnais's film work: "The cinema is made up of collaboration. That is why the question of knowing who is the author of a film is a question you can obviously ask yourself before beginning a film or from outside it, but one which happily never arises at all once shooting has begun."[30] The director remains the key figure, however, since it is he who co-ordinates the contributions of everyone else and is the only person present at every stage of the film-making, working successively with the writer, director of photography, actors, composer and editor and thereby supervising the film from the inception to the finished work. For the resolution of technical problems Resnais has kept to a single team: the continuity girl Sylvette Baudrot, director of photography Sacha Vierny and assistant Jean Léon have been with him since the beginning of his feature film work, the cameraman Philippe Brun since *Marienbad*. By contrast, he varies his writers and composers, as if afraid of being imprisoned within one style or method of approach. The case of the composer Pierre Barbaud is a par-

11

ticularly revealing instance of this[78]. He is a personal friend of Resnais who wrote the music for both *Le Mystère de l'Atelier Quinze* and *Le Chant du Styrène* and has a keen insight into Resnais's style and musical needs. Yet before they began their second collaboration, Resnais told him that, whatever the outcome, he would not ask him for another musical score. Resnais has adhered to this decision, though Barbaud has appeared as an actor in three of his four features.

Resnais's contribution to his films begins with the initial conception, since he insists on an original script ("I would not want to shoot the adaptation of a novel, because I think the writer has completely expressed himself in the novel and that wanting to make a film of it is a little like re-heating a meal"[30]) and generally provides the basic pattern — what he once called the 'algebraic conception of the work'[6] — within which the scriptwriter works. Resnais choses novelists rather than professional scriptwriters, because he is not interested in making films to a traditional recipe but does need a collaborator with both narrative gifts and 'a sense of spectacle'[38]. That he has a sure instinct for finding the latter is shown by the fact that Duras, Robbe-Grillet and Cayrol all went on to direct feature films after working with him. He always asks his writers "not to think about cinematic technique and to remain faithful to their own language"[38], setting himself the task of capturing the particular tone of the script, using the characters as his means of access. For all his films except *Marienbad* he has demanded from his writers detailed biographies and justifications of the characters' acts. Resnais also devotes great care to the shaping of his material into a dramatic pattern and, while the forms he adopts are always original, certain characteristics recur, such as the division of the action into five acts and the inclusion of an opening section designed to provoke and stimulate the spectator. This initial stage of film-making, from idea to finished script, is of vital importance to him: "I would find it very difficult to do without the pleasure of working with a writer who interests me: the interest of film-making lies precisely in seeing a film born, seeing the characters come to life, begin to contradict each other, escape us and refuse to say the phrases we want to make them pronounce; if all that is already printed, then obviously one does not have the same delight"[30].

The script evolved in this manner is normally shot with only minor alterations and the actual shooting is not the one essential creative moment of the film (as it is for Godard or Rossellini), rather it is "the elucidation of the script"[40]. Since spontaneity is not a prime concern for Resnais he can prepare the shooting beforehand, indeed, ideally he likes to explore the locations well in advance with his Leica and to hold a week or two of rehearsal with his players and his director of photography, so that as many of the problems of the film as possible can be seen and resolved in advance. Nowhere is Resnais's conception of the film as collaboration seen more clearly than in his work with his actors. Even a player with a tiny part is given a copy of the whole script and all are encouraged to contribute to the interpretation of the film. He has never been attracted by the idea of using non-professionals, simply because he has such a high regard for actors: "I have a great respect, a great love for the actor.

13

He has a very difficult and very delicate task and enormous demands are made on him"[21]. His methods of working reflect this attitude: "I never practise the technique of directing which consists in asking an actor for the opposite of what you want to obtain, knowing that by asking him for that you will make him do something else: generally actors are people sensitive and clever enough for you to be able to tell them the truth all the time".[30] From an actor's point of view he is a most stimulating and exciting director to work with, as Delphine Seyrig has made clear. On the one hand he grants the actor great autonomy: "From the moment he has chosen an actor he grants him his complete confidence. The actor is infallible in his eyes, he accepts him in his totality".[74] On the other, he makes enormous demands: "He likes to see just how far an actor can go, especially in a role he is not used to".[74]

Important as the scripting and shooting stages of the film are for Resnais, it is still true to say that the crucial stage is the editing. The pattern of the script and the style of the shooting are both determined by the possibilities of editing, which forms a third distinct phase of film-making. Just as the script is fixed before the shooting begins, so the shooting is finished before Resnais commences the editing. In conducting it Resnais is utterly ruthless, disregarding whether a shot was difficult or costly to obtain and removing any indication of the order of 'takes' so that a perfectly free choice can be made. His relationship with his editors forms a remarkable parallel to his collaboration with his authors. Henri Colpi who, with his wife Jasmine Chasney, edited both *Hiroshima mon Amour* and *Marienbad*, has given a fascinating

14

picture of Resnais's approach: "The first thing you should know about the editing of a film by Alain Resnais is that the labour in the cutting room does not begin with the breakdown of the first day's shooting but, quite the contrary, every foot of film remains untouched until the entire film has been shot. This method implies a great self-assurance in the course of shooting since no extra material or 'emergency' sequences are ever shot by Resnais, and this virtuoso method of working without cover indicates clearly that he has every intention of following the montage operation from A to Z. And, in fact, Resnais is constantly in the cutting room. He is always the first to arrive . . . yet he never touches either the film or the viewer. He never interferes unless we ask . . . and we ask him about even the tiniest problem which may come up".[51] As important as the montage of the images is the sound editing — the mixing of sound effects, dialogue and music — and equal care is lavished on this. It is in keeping with Resnais's whole philosophy of film-making that he has said that he would prefer the composer to be present from the very beginning of work on the film, although so far this has never been possible.

The characteristic of Resnais's filmic achievement is that he gives the cinema a new direction by ignoring what has been done before. At first sight this seems paradoxical: he had years of film viewing, film editing and short film making behind him when he made his first feature. He has a deep love for the silent cinema and his interest in the experimental period of the late twenties has been a lasting one. He said, for instance, of *Hiroshima mon Amour*: "Personally I thought

I had made an 'old-fashioned' film, in the style of 1930, with experiments in editing and cutting"[4]; and of *Marienbad:* "The action (one might say) seems to take place around 1930: I say 'seems': I wanted to renew a certain style of the silent cinema. The direction and the make-up try to recreate this atmosphere".[4] Yet in fact Resnais's films are wholly revolutionary, as was recognised from the beginning by the perceptive Jean-Luc Godard: "Seeing *Hiroshima,* you have the impression of seeing a film that is quite impossible to foresee in relation to what you already knew about the cinema"[93].

The explanation for this is twofold. All Resnais's writers have been literary men or women, not professional script-writers or film critics, so that the echoes one can find of, say, Louis Feuillade's film serials in *L'Année Dernière à Marienbad* are largely fortuitous. Robbe-Grillet, who conceived and wrote the whole film, is quite unacquainted with the early film-makers and Resnais himself does not believe in deliberate borrowing: "I believe that an influence ceases when the person receiving it becomes aware of it"[29]. Thus the Feuillade aspects of *Marienbad* are very different from the allusions to Louis Lumière in Godard's *Les Carabiniers* which are quite conscious and deliberate, forming a homage to the man and his work and reflecting Godard's own constant preoccupation with relating his own films to past filmic styles, genres and traditions. In the case of Godard, it is important to pick up such allusions, since the film relates more meaningfully to other films than to 'life' outside, but with Resnais only the visual texture of a film is likely to be influenced by his knowledge of film history, while the total effect is quite

16

without filmic precedent.

The refusal of mere imitation of the past is reinforced by Resnais's rejection of the notion that the pre-1930 cinema (the form of film-making that has influenced him most deeply) is somehow the 'real' cinema. However much he admires the achievements of the silent era, his own conception of the film medium is as something quite different: "A priori it seems to me that a film is always sound, talking and in colour. It is after this that you can try doing experiments, make a silent, black-and-white film for example"[5]. Elsewhere he has described the silent cinema as "an economic accident" and pointed out that "the people who invented photography and the cinema never thought for a moment that it could be in black-and-white: it happened like that and they were content with it, but it was not *normal*"[30]. Thus Resnais, rejecting the Kracauerian assumption that the film is an outgrowth of black-and-white photography, also opposes methods that aim at capturing the surface of life: "The realist cinema, the reconstruction of daily life, the reproduction of gestures, all that does not interest me at all."[4] Whereas for the realist film-maker the crucial stage is the actual shooting, for Resnais it is the editing when the elements are synthesised, image related to image and to voice, sound and music, so that the film becomes "a combination of a visual rhythm and a sound rhythm."[30]

It is in the light of this that we must view Resnais's concern with music and his avowed interest in an 'operatic' form of cinema, as well as his taste for literary commentaries and texts. The attempt at a new balance of word and image should not be viewed as a form of literary cinema. The films of

17

Resnais are certainly literate, in that their texts are written by professional writers creating a script with the same seriousness they would apply to a novel, and these texts are meaningful in a published form. But the films themselves, *Marienbad* for instance, are not literary since the particular effects achieved are impossible outside the cinema. Much of what we consider to be 'normal' film-making — the Italian neo-realist movement for example — uses narrative techniques derived essentially from nineteenth century literature. It is arguable that a form of film-making that does without such conventional literary concepts as 'plot' and 'character' is less, not more, literary. Certainly such concepts were evolved in works designed to show man's relationship with his fellows in society (and were therefore so successfully taken over by the Italian film-makers of the forties whose preoccupations were much the same), but they are of little use to a film-maker like Resnais who has been concerned since his first documentary with what happens in the mind far more than what happens in society. Resnais is akin to the literary modernists in this preoccupation with new forms and stylistic patterns, but he does not ape literature; rather, he expands our conception of the capacities of cinematic expression.

2. The Shaping of a Film-Maker

> *L'influence la plus profonde est peut-être celle qui ne laisse aucune trace visible.*
> ALAIN RESNAIS

A LAIN RESNAIS was born on June 3, 1922, at Vannes in the department of Morbihan in Britanny, where his father — like the father of the actress in *Hiroshima mon Amour* — was a chemist. He attended the Catholic school of Saint-François-Xavier as a day boy, but his films lack any concern with religious issues. As he himself once put it: "I don't refuse the next world. I simply state that it is outside my range and I prefer to attack what I can change"[5]. In any case his progress was hampered by ill-health — he suffered from attacks of asthma — and in 1936, when he was fourteen, his mother took him away from school and devoted herself to his education at home. Childhood friends of his — the Hilleret brothers — have given us a picture of the young Alain: "For us he was someone apart. Always with his nose in books. We envied him because he could do as he liked. He had an extraordinary bicycle with every imaginable accessory ... And then there was his camera and above all his 8 mm ciné camera."[43] One of his early passions was for comics: "Often too we went to Aradon, on the gulf of Morbihan, where his parents had a property. It was there that he kept his monstrous collection of comics and 'space-operas'. He had everything which could possibly exist in that field. He was immobile, asthmatic, and no doubt he found there the opportunity of escaping into imaginary space."[43]

It was to his mother that Alain owed his first taste for

literature. Gaston Bounoure[97], to whom we are indebted for most of our knowledge of the young Resnais, records that it was at the age of fourteen that he discovered Proust and such authors as Aldous Huxley and Katherine Mansfield. One of his earliest teenage film projects was an adaptation of 'Brave New World' and much later, around 1945, one of his first (and most disappointing) professional assignments was as cameraman and editor on a 16mm short directed by Jean Leduc called *Le Sommeil* (or *Les Yeux) d'Albertine*, based on an incident in Proust's great novel.

Resnais has retained his love of literature and music. His conception of film construction owes much to music and he has himself spoken of his debt to Stravinsky[5], while his literary tastes are clearly revealed in his "mania for demanding texts that are 'too literary' "[6] in his shorts, and his collaboration with novelists on feature films. Projects for films that have never been realised show the same bias. In 1951, for example, he contemplated adaptations of 'Pierrot mon Ami' ("I have always had an enormous passion for Raymond Queneau and if one day I was fortunate enough to work with him, whatever he might do would inevitably please me since I can even think that my films are influenced by him"[30]) and 'Les Mauvais Coups' ("Vailland was a sort of god for me, a youthful passion. I would have liked to shoot one of his novels, 'Les Mauvais Coups' for example. But that was not the time to make such films; I only made shorts and producers were afraid."[4])

The effects of these influences are hard to determine and certainly Queneau is not a name that would immediately spring to mind if one were considering Resnais's work, but this is a constant feature with him: the influences that contribute most to the shaping of his sensibilities remain largely hidden. One interest that has been with him since a very early age is the cinema and Resnais has himself described his first contact with it: "I'm often tempted to say that the three films that marked me most were the first three I saw. The first was a documentary on the growth of a bean: you could see a bean grow, develop, open, it was extraordinary; with it there was one of Harold Lloyd's films, I think, called *Le Château Hanté*, and the third was a cartoon by Lortac called *Le Lever du Professeur Mecanicas*, a science fiction cartoon. They were projected by my cousin on a towel in the sitting room, and it was from that moment on that I began going to look in dustbins for boxes which I opened and passed rolls of paper through, saying to myself: 'It's a camera, it's a camera'. "[30] This first contact was soon extended: "Afterwards, there must have been the Pathéorama films: there were film serials, Gance's *Napoléon*, for example. Then I had a piece of film that I used to show myself all the time under the piano: it lasted two minutes and you could see galloping horses' hooves, a mysterious stranger turning his head, a lady dressed in white lace holding a pair of opera-glasses and accompanied by a gentleman in a top-hat; I saw this film hundreds of times and it was not until almost thirty-five years later that I saw Renoir's *Nana* at the Cinémathèque and suddenly shouted out: 'That's my piece!' So I could say I was very much influenced by Renoir"[30]. If the first film show was a decisive date in Alain Resnais's development

21

there are also several others one can discern: at ten, at thirteen and again at fifteen he had important formative experiences.

The young Alain's normal childhood interest in comics has already been mentioned. Francis Lacassin puts 1932 as the year when this interest became something deeper. It was in Paris, on the steps of the Madeleine, that the ten-year-old Alain bought a copy of the 'Sunday News' and discovered that the comics he had devoured with such enthusiasm were merely pale copies of American originals. At the same time he also made his first contact with Dick Tracy, subsequently to become his favourite strip-cartoon character. On another visit to Paris five years later he went to the editorial office of the French comic magazines 'Robinson' and 'Mickey' and on his return to Vannes persuaded his father to subscribe to American newspapers. All the time he built up his collection of comics so that it was eventually to become one of the finest in France. This passion for comics has persisted: in Paris after the Liberation he came to know other enthusiasts, like Chris Marker and Remo Forlani, both of whom became close associates. In 1962 he was elected vice-president of the organisation which began as the 'Club des Bandes Dessinées' but was subsequently renamed, at his suggestion, the 'Centre d'Etude des Littératures d'Expression Graphique'. He also joined the editorial committee of 'Giff-Wiff', the first magazine devoted entirely to the study of comics, and to both functions he brings an unrivalled knowledge. Francis Lacassin says of him: "Thanks to the sureness of his memory and the selective quality of his collections he is among us all the one who knows in the most erudite fashion the history of the comic strip."[64]

Explicit references to, or borrowings from the world of comics are quite hard to find in Resnais's work. Several of his projects with Remo Forlani drew on this world — including a feature-length film on the adventures of Tin-Tin — but none of these came to fruition. Resnais's eternal project, *Les Aventures d'Harry Dickson*, based on Jean Ray's master detective in vogue around 1932, has likewise never been realised and the film which reveals the taste for comics most clearly, *Toute la mémoire du monde*, does so only in the form of a few asides and tiny hints to the cognoscenti, such as the listing of Chester Gould, creator of Dick Tracy, as one of the collaborators. On the surface, the influence is small, yet Resnais expressed his surprise when in 1960 Max Egly commented on this predilection for comics: "But they are a world of their own, comics. You talk about comics as if, seeing me reading a novel, you were to say: 'I see! you like literature'. "[7] Resnais continued: "What I know about the cinema, I have learned as much through comics as through the cinema"[7].

The importance of comics to Resnais's work is twofold. Firstly, they represent a non-realistic method of narrative, using such processes as distortion, isolation of a character from his setting and violent colour contrast for dramatic ends. They also frequently have a 'commentary' quite separately narrating the events in the form of the line or two of print underneath. But above all they give an illusion of movement, flow and action through the linking of static pictures, so that, as Resnais himself has said: "The rules of the shooting-script and of editing are the same in comics as in the cinema."[7]

23

Certainly it can hardly have been chance that when Resnais began to work professionally in the cinema it was as an editor and that his first 35mm films were films on art, involving the animation of pre-existing pictorial material (the paintings of Van Gogh, Gauguin and Picasso). As Chris Marker pointed out at the time, it is not because Resnais's camera moves that these art films are real films. It is because of the way in which he pieces the shots together by editing, in the case of *Guernica*, for example, recreating in time a vision that already existed in space, that is to say making a motion picture out of a static painting.

Another important date in the young Resnais's life was in 1935 when, at the age of thirteen, he made his first film. As he tells us, the experiment was not altogether successful: "Unfortunately I had set out on a very shaky foundation. I had begun to shoot a version of *Fantômas* and I thought that since the actors were children, I only needed to bring the camera up closer to make them look like adults. But when the film was projected, it did not work out at all. I was plunged into despair and the actors were discouraged. It was nothing unusual at the time to shoot 8mm films. The originality was to shoot with people."[5] The choice of subject matter for this film is also significant. The master criminal Fantômas, drawn from the popular novels of Pierre Souvestre and Marcel Allain and made still more famous in 1913 by the film version directed by Louis Feuillade, belongs to the same sub-literary vein as Harry Dickson and Dick Tracy. The only other of Resnais's youthful films known to us by name is *L'Aventure de Guy*, made about the same time from a script by the actor Gaston Modot which he had found in a magazine and no doubt retitled in honour of another of his strip-cartoon heroes, Guy l'Eclair (The Flash). There were certainly many others too and Georges Hilleret has given us a fascinating glimpse of the future director at work: "His great pleasure ... was to go and take up position in the Rue de la Salle d'Asile (a street which has not changed since the middle ages, tortuous, ill-paved and with a gutter running down the middle of the roadway) or behind the Corn Hall, to photograph unawares with his 8mm camera the little girls he knew from the girls' school. When these films were developed, he used to invite his friends — boys and girls — to come and see them. In a little room he had installed a projection room that was uncomfortable but fitted out with real wooden cinema seats that we used to clatter happily whenever we got up."[43] This habit of making private or personal films was taken up again by Resnais, this time in 16mm, after he went to Paris, and continued until about 1948 when his professional work began to absorb too much of his time.

A third decisive encounter that helped to shape Alain Resnais's development took place in 1937 when he was on a visit to Paris. It was "a performance of Chekhov's 'The Seagull' given by the Pitoëffs in 1937 at the Théâtre des Mathurins. The most curious thing is that I thought I did not like the theatre. Then, suddenly, it became the most important thing in the world for me. So much so, that I decided to become an actor! ... I was fifteen years old."[3] In 1940, as soon as he had obtained his baccalauréat he left Vannes for Paris where he joined the Cours René Simon to study acting for two years. These early years in Paris were marked by disappointment and uncertainty — at one time he even thought of giving up both the theatre and cinema and becoming a librarian — but finally he did come to focus his talents on film-making. Danièle Delorme, who knew him as a fellow student at the acting course, has given us a clear picture of Resnais at this period of his life: "I retain the memory of a person apart, who observed, watched and did not say anything. I never saw him on the stage or presenting anything at all. No. But with him, outside the course, we talked, discussed a lot. He was, for some of us, a rallying point. At that time he lived somewhere at the end of the Rue de Courcelles. We used to meet in his room, and on his projector he would show us old films, *Metropolis* for example. We used to accompany these old films with music. Things like 'The Firebird': These meetings were important for us"[45]. After completing the course, Resnais did not go on to the stage immediately and it was not until 1945, when he was doing his military service, that he joined a theatrical company, 'Les Arlinquins', directed by André Voisin. He was with the company for about a year and a half, spending fourteen months at Schönberg in Austria where the company led a communal life, acting, training, rehearsing. Resnais did research, read manuscripts and acted small parts in the plays produced — a gendarme in Ghéon's 'Le Pendu dépendu' and Don Basile in 'The Barber of Seville', for example. André Voisin has given this judgement on Alain Resnais the actor: "Alain wanted to become an actor, really. But he only wanted to be a very good one. He had some doubts and these prevented him from letting himself go. He suffered because of it. But he brought a lot of seriousness to his interpretations. A personal note too, not very classical but always valuable."[44] Resnais's own verdict was somewhat harsher: "As the results did not really correspond to what I dreamed of, I gave up being an actor."[3]

Resnais's first real contact with the stage ended in failure but the theatre was not without its effect on him. It remained his favourite milieu and one reason why he began to make films in the years 1946-8 was to keep in contact with actors. What troubled him most when he became a documentary film-maker was the lack of actors and it was to compensate for this that he used men and women from the theatre to speak the commentaries of his short films. When he was finally in a position to make feature films, it was to the theatre he turned to find such actresses as Emmanuelle Riva and Delphine Seyrig. On a deeper level too Resnais's film style is characterised by theatrical acting. His aim is to deny the audience any too-easy identification with the players: "Let us say that I am concerned to address the spectator in a critical state of mind. For that I need to make films that are not natural"[4]. Actresses like Riva and Seyrig make this possible: "If I turn to actors from the theatre it is undoubtedly because I am looking for a kind of realism that is not 'realism', and I look for actors who can give a certain type of intonation, a certain phrasing more difficult to obtain from actors trained in the cinema."[41] Apart from Agnès Varda, it is difficult to think of other film directors who have employed quite this approach to acting, but the theatrical parallel is immediate

27

and striking. Bert Brecht with his 'epic' theatre and theory of alienation *(Verfremdungseffekt)* is clearly exploring a similar path. Resnais became acquainted with Brecht's theories after the Liberation and would certainly favour the application to the cinema of Brecht's dictum that "Our theatre must encourage the thrill of comprehension and train people in the pleasure of changing reality."

As we have seen from Danièle Delorme's words, Resnais retained in Paris his interest in the cinema, showing silent films to his friends. He also went often to the cinema just as he had gone every Thursday as a schoolboy in Vannes, and it has been suggested that he may have been strongly influenced by the kind of French films he saw during the Occupation years (which were his first in Paris), when the French cinema was forced away from direct confrontation with reality into the stylistic experiment of *Les Visiteurs du Soir* and *Les Dames du Bois de Boulogne*. The early passion has persisted and in 1960 he estimated that he saw about eighty to a hundred films a year and, asked about the directors who had influenced him, replied: "Certainly, at one and the same time and in some way: Buñuel, Cocteau's *Orphée*, Antonioni, then Welles and then Eisenstein, Visconti . . . If there is an influence, it is at one and the same time very precise and very subterranean. But how can you know?"[5] One important name that does not appear in this list is Sacha Guitry, of whom Resnais has spoken elsewhere[6].

Such a wealth of names reveals both a wide knowledge of the cinema and a fairly eclectic taste. What these directors do have in common, however, is a dissatisfaction with the conception of the cinema as the direct recording of reality, and Resnais's tastes, like his own films, move more in the direction of a cinema that plays with the possibilities of tracking shot and commentary (Guitry's *Le Roman d'un Tricheur*), that is theatrical *(White Nights)*, operatic (Eisenstein's *Alexander Nevsky)* and unreal *(Orphée)*. At the same time films like *Muriel* and *La Guerre est finie* are rooted in real life and many of his collaborators have spoken of his quest for realism: "His décor and accessories are always seen in a realist perspective"[71] (Jacques Saulnier, his art director), "With Resnais, the conception of the whole is always realistic"[73] (Philippe Brun, his cameraman), "When we rehearsed in the corridors of the hotel [for *Marienbad*] it was always with the idea of finding the simplest, most natural gesture"[74] (Delphine Seyrig). Also, when he is shooting on location, fidelity to his setting is axiomatic for Resnais: "Even when I am concerned with an element of décor I would not like to transform it for the camera. It is up to the camera to find a way of bringing the décor out in the required manner, it is not up to the décor to bow to the camera."[40] In fact there is no real discrepancy here, for as the example of Visconti shows realism and theatricality can go side by side. Perhaps Resnais himself defined most clearly his own particular style when he pointed out that besides the traditions of Méliès and Lumière there exists that of Louis Feuillade, which "marvellously utilises the fantasy of Méliès and the realism of Lumière"[29]. His tribute to Feuillade (whom he discovered in 1944) shows his own attachment to this form of cinema: "I would be very proud to be influenced by Feuillade and if

29

his imprint were to be found in my films, I should be enormously pleased. For Feuillade is much more for me than a classic — I hardly like to apply this title to him on account of its academic sound — he is one of my gods: the one who has accomplished what I have long dreamed of."[29]

Resnais's early interest in the cinema was not only that of a spectator. When his acting course ended he enrolled in 1943 at the Institut des Hautes Etudes Cinématographiques (IDHEC) where he began a course in editing which he later abandoned after only eighteen months, largely because the tuition was too theoretical. His meeting with the editress Myriam led to his first professional work as assistant editor on Nicole Védrès's compilation film *Paris 1900* (1947). This concern with editing, growing so naturally out of his interest in the narrative methods of the comic strip, persisted. He edited all his own short films, worked for a number of other directors, and only finally abandoned editing when he became a feature director — up till then his careers as short-film director and editor ran side by side — and since he once went so far as to say that he only became a film director because he could not get enough work as an editor, it would be wrong to underestimate the importance of this stage of his career.

Of all the films, apart from his own, that he edited, the most important is undoubtedly *La Pointe Courte*, in which the twenty-seven-year-old Agnès Varda astonishingly anticipated many aspects of the later Resnais style, including a theme of troubled love, a part-theatrical, part-documentary tone and the placing of the lovers against an alien setting. Varda

30

herself has given a valuable picture of Resnais's approach to this film and the whole question of editing in general: "At that time the only film of Alain's I knew was *Guernica*. That was enough for me to dare ask him to edit *La Pointe Courte* which I had just shot instinctively, intuitively, as a revolt, an isolated act. I sent him the script. He replied immediately in a very long and attentive letter. He explained that it was just not possible for him: this cinema corresponded too closely to what he dreamed of doing himself. All the same he accepted a little later. The editing was very slow, six months, here in this very room [Varda's flat in the Rue Daguerre] where we had installed a hired viewing machine. We lived here. For the others Resnais had disappeared. For me it was a time of reflection. Like an apprenticeship in the kind of cinema I had to continue, in which Alain was able to give me confidence. When he could have arranged things, made them follow his own inclination, he did nothing of the sort. He wanted above all to leave me responsible for my errors and also for a certain personal accent. That is his integrity. Thanks to him I understood my own work. By scrupulously editing my film he allowed me to clarify my own thoughts. And he sent me to the cinema — I hardly ever went at that time — made me really love it. Yes, that was a vital encounter for me and if he did not have any direct influence on my first film, it is to him that I owe becoming what I now am."[46] These six months must have formed a key period in Resnais's own development too when many of his own views were tested and a basis for his future feature film work evolved.

But almost ten years before his collaboration with Varda,

Resnais had found the need to express himself by directing films. Already at Schönberg, André Voisin tells us[44], he used to film his fellow actors and little incidents in their life there. On his return to Paris this private film-making continued and in the years 1946 to 1948, immediately prior to the beginning of his professional career, he made quite a number of 16mm films of a far more personal kind than any he has made since. Unfortunately, virtually all of this work has been lost or destroyed and we have to rely on the testimony of some of those who participated in these film-making ventures or who were close friends of his at the time, if we are to capture the flavour of a largely unknown period of Resnais's life.

The first of these films, *Schéma d'une Identification* (1946), was made with a young actor who lived in the same apartment house as Resnais in the Rue du Dragon, whom he had seen in his first play at Cannes four years earlier and who was now on the brink of a brilliant international career: Gérard Philipe. Resnais's only recorded comments on this film, a surrealist experiment in which Gérard Philipe played a rake and François Chaumette a proletarian, are a tribute to his leading actor: "We shot the film in an unheated flat. He was never late. He had an extraordinary professional conscience. I was struck by the extent to which he had taken the thing seriously, as if he were working for René Clair. When we were working, from the moment we had agreed on the interpretation and the movements, everything remained fixed to the very millimetre. Never were we more in contact than then."[97] This ability to obtain from others a degree of seriousness equal to his own has been a constant feature of Resnais's career as a director and the secret of his successful use of the method of collaboration.

Ouvert pour cause d'Inventaire (1946), a second lost work, was a feature-length film starring Danièle Delorme, Nadine Alari and Pierre Trabaud, for which two other provisional titles are known: *Assieds-toi, veux-tu, dans la bergère* and *Affaire classée*. Resnais's own comment on it is: "The first feature-length film I made, which is heaven knows where today, was on Paris. I shot it in 16mm during 1946. I wanted to express what I had discovered at the age of twelve. It was a sort of diary; later that sort of thing was called 'caméra-stylo' "[12] [Alexandre Astruc's term for the new, personal style of cinema, "a means of writing as supple and subtle as that of written language"]. The film was, Danièle Delorme tells us, "an escapade in Paris, with an old raincoat which we were running after all the time. An old raincoat, all dirty and worn"[45]. Agnès Varda, to whom Resnais showed the film, remembers it rather better: "It was not a film that you can recount easily. Only a succession of pure sensations which never really reach the state of consciousness. An attempt to illustrate that silent world — fear, desire — which you cannot really define"[46]. Delorme remembers the film being shot "near the Canal St. Martin. There was a succession of bistrots, cafés"[45]. And Varda: "The quarter Bolivar, the Buttes-Chaumont: a nerve centre for Resnais. It was there that his grandfather the chemist lived. I think one must respect the adolescent character of this film, above all not try to explain it. It's too close to that zone of unavowable sensibility. It was the film of a provincial fascinated by Paris,

33

by the approach to the city."[46] Without a viewing of the film it is impossible to estimate its exact place in Resnais's work but it is fair to assume that it contained the germ of much of his later work. There is, for example, in Resnais's eyes at least, a link with *L'Année Dernière à Marienbad*. Questioned about the artificial poses of the background figures in this latter film, Resnais said: "As a child one of the things that struck me most were the motionless people at the street corners who were waiting for heaven knows what . . . Besides I made a film, in 16mm, about this subject where you could see, in that way, people frozen at the corner of the Rue des Plantes. And this film, for me, asked the question, 'What can there be in the heads of these people I pass every day?' "[39]

1947 was another year filled with 16mm film-making. *L'Alcool tue* was conceived by Paul Renty (one of André Bazin's assistants at 'Travail et Culture' — the other was Chris Marker) and produced by Renty's wife Christiane. The film, originally intended to be a western, was inspired by a quarry the Rentys found on a family picnic near Meaux. The script was worked out one Sunday with Remo Forlani and Roland Dubillard and shot in two days at the cost of about 15,000 francs. It was about a priest who, concerned at the drinking of the workmen in the quarry, saves their souls by banging them over the head with a crucifix and despatching them in a truck direct to heaven. The truck and rails allowed Resnais, who was both director and cameraman, to include some tracking shots, and he edited it himself in his flat in the Rue des Plantes. The only showing it received was in Resnais's bathroom. Remo Forlani, with whom Resnais was to make *Toute la mémoire du monde* nine years later, also collaborated on a project to be called *Campagne Première*, a reportage on the painters living in a street of that name in Paris. Forlani, however, was called up for military service and Resnais, left on his own, made instead a series of 16mm silent visits to individual painters. He also made at this time several other films known to us only by name: *Portrait d'Henri Goetz*, *La Bague*, a mime drama featuring Marcel Marceau who had been a fellow member of the 'Arlinquins' troupe, and a first colour film *Journée Naturelle*, also known as *Visite à Max Ernst*.

The following year was to see Resnais join the ranks of professional film-makers but it too began with more work of a semi-private kind. For Paul Renty he began another film, a documentary written by Roland Dubillard on *Les Jardins de Paris*, but this was abandoned after about 1,500 metres of negative had been shot. Completely on his own he made a short composed of still photographs of the tourist monuments, *Châteaux de France*, which he financed himself and for which he collected material on a bicycle with his camera on his back. More important, however, were two films on art he made with Gaston Diehl, *Van Gogh* and *Malfray*, for the first of these was seen by the producer Pierre Braunberger, who commissioned him to remake it in 35mm, and so begin his 'official' career as a documentarist.

3. The Documentary Years

> *Tous mes films ont été des films de commande. Il ne faut donc pas me considérer comme quelqu'un — si seulement je pouvais être de ceux-là — qui aurait un message à délivrer au monde.*
> ALAIN RESNAIS

IN 1948, at the age of twenty-six, Resnais began a career as documentarist that was to last ten years, in which time he directed seven shorts and collaborated closely on the making of another. In one sense this period represents a long detour for the director who, after all, had come to Paris initially to become an actor and whose film-making had, from the very first, implied working with actors. Yet now, for a decade, he had to work solely with paintings, documents, buildings. Naturally he was attracted to feature film-making, but none of his projects came to fruition and he was forced to remain a documentarist and to develop his style in short films, partly because of the belief — common among French producers in the early fifties — that short film makers could not successfully make feature films, and partly because of his own intransigence. In 1957, for example, he turned down the chance to make a film version of Hervé Bazin's novel *La Tête contre les Murs*. There is a certain ironic ring about Resnais's reasons for refusing: "After *Nuit et Brouillard* and *Toute la mémoire du monde* I was afraid of shutting myself up in a lunatic asylum, in a new concentration camp universe. That was becoming obsessive, always walls, always prisons."[5] Four years later he was directing *L'Année Dernière à Marienbad*, the hermetic film *par excellence* and one in which the leading character says at one point: "There were always walls — everywhere around me — smooth, even, varnished, without the least break, there were always walls..."

In all his film work Resnais constantly searches for new forms: "I want to make films that are experiments. All experiments are interesting."[4] This implies a refusal of anything that seems like a mere repetition, yet despite this Resnais's work does have a unity. On the surface his short films form a heterogeneous agglomeration: films on art and the Spanish Civil War, negro culture, the concentration camps and the French national library, the prevention of accidents and the manufacture of polystyrene. All were commissioned works on themes suggested by producers, yet when one looks at them closely it is apparent that they are linked and that gradually, from film to film, Resnais evolves his method of collaboration, lays down the basis of his style and clarifies his personal attitude to the issues raised. Above all the films are linked by the seriousness of mind with which each commission is approached: "I tried not to cheat, not to use trickery in my shorts. There was the commission and I was intent on respecting it."[3]

VAN GOGH (1948)

Alain Resnais's documentary career began with two films on art. As he admitted to François Truffaut in an interview published in 1956[10], Resnais is not the 'father of the art film' and the late forties are in fact a time of great activity in this genre in France. Resnais himself mentions two debts: the obvious one to Luciano Emmer, the documentarist (and later feature film director) who pioneered the art film in Italy, and a more 'personal' debt to Chester Gould. This explicit reference to the creator of Dick Tracy in connection with his art films bears out the importance already stressed of the comic strip as source of Resnais's editing and film-making styles. *Van Gogh* also marks the establishment of Resnais's method of collaboration — whereas his 'private' films had been made independently, all his commissioned 35mm works were made in co-operation with writers, in this case Robert Hessens and Gaston Diehl. The film *Van Gogh* is divided into four sections, corresponding to the main stages of the painter's six years of full self-realisation as an artist which were, simultaneously, years bringing him ever nearer to death.

One of the reasons why *Van Gogh* is so interesting is that in 1948, in 'Ciné-Club No. 3' Resnais published a statement of his aims in this film, which remains his only written analysis of his own work. The title of the article, 'An Experiment', indicates the attitude with which the shooting was approached. The particular question involved in the film was in fact, "to find out whether painted trees, painted people, painted houses could, thanks to editing, fulfil the role of real objects and whether, in this case, it was possible to substitute for the spectator and almost without his knowing it, the interior world of the artist in place of the world as it is revealed by photography"[1]. There are several aspects of this statement that call for comment. Firstly, Resnais did not begin his documentary career by taking his camera out into the real world, as any conventional realist film-maker would do, but looked instead for a substitute for photographic reality.

Secondly, the means of integration and substitution was the process of editing, which is the key to the success of *Van Gogh* and remains the corner-stone of Resnais's mature style. It is in the light of these considerations that one can interpret the director's manipulation of the material of Van Gogh's paintings, which appear on the screen more or less in the order in which they were painted and which form the film's only visual reality (there are no photographs of real landscapes). The content of Van Gogh's paintings is selected and fused in the same way that a director might deal with real settings: the camera tracks towards a window in the picture 'La maison jaune', then the director cuts to an interior window from which the camera gradually draws back to reveal Van Gogh's room ('La chambre à coucher de l'artiste à Arles'). Similarly there is a tracking shot into a painting of the St. Rémy asylum (so that we seem, like Van Gogh, to be going along the corridor and up to the door) followed by a cut to the violent Provençal landscape that seems to hit us in the eye as it hit Van Gogh. The story to be told in the film is dramatic enough and Van Gogh's paintings are sufficiently powerful to survive the kind of distortion inevitable with this approach. In the case of one spectator at least Resnais's ambitions were fully and totally fulfilled, since he received a letter from a lady who wrote to say how splendid the film was and how he must have enjoyed travelling to all those places painted by Van Gogh![40]

The choice of subject-matter is also significant. As Resnais says, the film is not art criticism or scientific biography but 'an attempt to tell the imaginary life of a painter through his painting."[10] It tries to put us in Van Gogh's head and let us see the world not as it literally appeared to him (the photographic reality) but as it is transmuted by his vision (what is captured on his canvases). In this undertaking Resnais is aided by the series of devastatingly honest self-portraits that Van Gogh painted between 1885 and 1890 and by the very nature of the painter's brushwork which together reveal so graphically the progressive collapse of his grip on life. This interest in an interior or mental world is one that occurs again and again in Resnais's work which, from one point of view, might be seen as a rebuttal of Jacques Prévert's assertion (in 'Paroles'):

"Quand on le laisse seul
Le monde mental
Ment
Monumentalement."

Some of the parallels between *Van Gogh* and *Marienbad* are quite striking: in neither film do we get outside the images of mental life and into the fresh air of a real landscape, and Gaston Diehl's evocation, in the commentary, of the St. Rémy asylum is a striking anticipation of the gardens of *Marienbad:* "A garden surrounded by walls ... an unusual silence ... an agonising calm ... a nature where everything becomes a portent."

To unify his material Resnais used two principal means. Firstly, he chose to make the film in black and white which allowed him to "create links between extremely disparate canvases" and, as André Bazin has pointed out[95], to treat the whole of the painter's output as a single immense picture.

The vigour of Van Gogh's brushwork and the compelling quality of his vision allowed the paintings to survive monochrome reproduction, and the qualities that have led to the kind of disparagement sometimes made of Van Gogh, that he "remained all his life a draughtsman" or that his ideas "were only black and white ideas" (two criticisms recorded, and partially refuted by Herbert Read) in fact helped rather than hindered Resnais. A second and more positive means of linking the canvases was by the use of the musical score written by Jacques Besse. "The multiplicity of the shots (almost as many as in a feature film) forced us," Resnais wrote, "to give the music a predominant importance. It is no longer there to 'accompany the images' but to create the very backbone of the film"[1]. Where *Van Gogh* differs from most of Resnais's shorts is in the lack of interest of its commentary which in his later work came to be a further linking element. Here Gaston Diehl's commentary is flat, matter-of-fact, occasionally falling into cliché and never achieving the kind of heightening of language needed to encompass the climaxes of Van Gogh's life (his mad act of self-immolation at Arles, his suicide at Anvers) for which direct pictorial evidence is of necessity lacking.

GAUGUIN (1950)

Resnais's second and much shorter documentary is almost universally regarded as his least interesting work and is the only one he himself has ever virtually rejected. Again working with Gaston Diehl, but this time without Hessens, Resnais probed the life of another tormented member of the post-

41

impressionist generation, Paul Gauguin, who was not mentioned in *Van Gogh* although he was closely connected with the Dutch painter and a witness to the acts of madness at Arles. In its externals, this film tells much the same story as *Van Gogh:* another journey undertaken by a painter in search of himself, his style and the sun, which again led to disappointment. In Gauguin's case the goal was Tahiti and the result dire poverty and nostalgia for home (symbolised by the painting of a snow-covered Breton landscape which Paul Gauguin took with him on his last voyage to the South Seas and which, according to legend, was found on his easel after his death). The methods used in *Gauguin* to tell this tale were precisely those of the earlier documentary but this time the material did not lend itself to filming in black-and-white. Whereas Van Gogh was a draughtsman, Gauguin was a colourist, a man who once said: "Everything must be sacrificed to pure colour," and who described his paintings as "symphonies, harmonies that represent nothing absolutely *real.*" The economic circumstances that compelled Resnais to shoot in black-and-white a film he could only conceive of in colour were largely responsible for the resulting failure, and the director was not helped by a musical score written by Darius Milhaud that tended to drown the pictures rather than to link them. But above all *Gauguin* was only a repetition of what Resnais had done before: "For a film to interest me, it must have an experimental side; that is what was lacking in *Gauguin* and that is why it is a bad film."[5] Since 1950 Resnais has never attempted to repeat a success, either by adopting again methods that he himself has already successfully applied or by adapting an existing novel or literary work to the screen. He has remained true to his belief in experiment.

GUERNICA (1950)

Undeterred by this failure, Resnais made a third art film, this time with Robert Hessens, who conceived the idea of the film, as co-director. Picasso's enormous fresco 'Guernica' has distinct advantages over Paul Gauguin's paintings as the subject for a black-and-white documentary, since it uses only black, white and gradations of grey. But the problems it posed were nonetheless real, for the subject-matter is vast and difficult to encompass in a short film of just over three hundred metres. *Guernica*, despite its considerable achievement, showed Resnais striving to get beyond the confines of the art film, for it is the destruction and suffering caused by war that forms the real subject of the film *Guernica*, not Pablo Picasso's technique or style. Indeed the painter's name is never mentioned in the film except in an initial note to the effect that the film was realised with the aid of paintings, drawings and sculptures which Picasso executed between 1902 and 1949. Resnais's interest is in the subject-matter of the painting: "Guernica seemed to us the manifestation of the will to destroy for the pleasure of destroying: making an experiment on human material, just to see. That begins with Guernica and you can see where it all ends."[2] In all his films Resnais approaches his documents with a desire for complete honesty and seeks an authentic voice to accompany them: just as the text of *Gauguin* was taken from the painter's own letters and the script of *Nuit et Brouillard* written by a victim of the concentration camps, so here, in *Guernica*, Resnais turned for his commentary to the poet Paul Eluard who had been Picasso's most frequent visitor in 1937 when work on the painting was in progress and whose poem 'The Victory of Guernica' dates from the same time.

The film *Guernica* opens with a photograph of the ruins of the town and a calm statement of facts, very much in the manner of the 'Times' report of the bombing and spoken by a man's voice. Reference is made to Guernica's position as cultural centre of the Basques, its sacred oak, the events of April 26, 1937 when three and a half hours of bombing and machine-gunning resulted in two thousand deaths. This section concludes with the reason for this attack: "to find out the effect of combined explosive and incendiary bombing on a civilian population." Then the image changes to Picasso paintings of 1901-6 (his blue period): clowns, acrobats, women, children; and the calm grave voice of the tragedienne Maria Casarès replaces the more matter-of-fact diction of the man to intone Paul Eluard's poetic lines: "Poor sacrificed faces, your death will serve as an example". Now the full horror is introduced with words that anticipate the opening of *Hiroshima:* "We read everything in the newspapers". Shots of *graffiti* and newspaper headlines with words like war, fascism, Guernica, resistance picked out, are used to reinforce Picasso paintings, all riddled with bullets: "To think that so many of us were afraid of lightning, afraid of thunder." Then shots of suffering faces (of the kind Picasso painted so frequently around 1937) and the sound of aeroplanes herald the first shots of the painting 'Guernica': alternating flashes of the lamp and darkness to simulate an explosion. While Picasso's painting lets us see the suffering victims, Eluard's text gives us the appearance of the aggressors: "Helmeted, booted, well behaved, handsome lads, the airmen drop their bombs methodically." On the ground the "disgusting harvest" continues — men and animals, wounded and suffering: "Go and hold back a beast that smells death. Go and explain to a mother the death of her child . . . There is only one night, that of war."

Over images of death and desolation, the commentary continues: "You are food for worms and crows, yet you were our quivering hope." There is no clear image of hope in Picasso's painting, the emphasis there, as in most of his paintings around that time, was on suffering and anguish, but the film does not accept this as a final comment. Using a Picasso sculpture of 1944, 'L'Homme au Mouton', it finds a note of hope: "Beneath the dead wood of the oak of Guernica, on the ruins of Guernica, under the pure sky of Guernica, a man has returned bearing in his arms a bleating kid and in his heart a dove." His message fills the screen and gives the film its ending: "Guernica, innocence will overcome crime, Guernica!"

Whereas the works of Van Gogh and Gauguin were fused to make a single whole, in the film *Guernica* one painting is broken down into jagged, isolated fragments, each representing an image of suffering. The film can disregard the spatial organisation of the painting (which is never shown in its entirety) because it recreates the elements in a temporal sequence which, thanks to the editing, acquires its own rhythm. Hessens and Resnais were able to fuse other Picasso works (early ones for innocence, the 1944 sculpture for hope) with 'Guernica' and its related studies of suffering, because the painting, though begun within a week of the massacre and given a definite political purpose, uses Picasso's own personal imagery — horses, bulls, women — in place of particularised images of a specific 1937 disaster. The importance of Guy Bernard's music and Paul Eluard's text, spoken by Maria Casarès, cannot be overestimated. Here a sober text, completely in the manner of the opening statement, would have clashed with the images, yet words were obviously needed to give the context of Picasso's painting which is itself an image of pure suffering with no aggressors, no planes, no bullets. Eluard's mixture of poetry and prose captures exactly the right note, reinforcing the painting's suffering lament and adding its own hymn to love and hope, seeing Guernica not simply as a place of terrible suffering but as one of the 'capitals of living peace.' In some ways this message anticipates Resnais's later work where love is opposed to suffering and the city of Hiroshima becomes a place where love is found and experienced. Stylistically too *Guernica* represents for the director the first totally successful fusion of all the elements on which his mature style is based. Fragments of photographs, painting and sculpture are welded into a visual rhythm and set against an aural rhythm of music and verbal poetry bound together in a tone that combines documentary realism with pure lyricism.

LES STATUES MEURENT AUSSI (1950 - 53)

Resnais's fourth documentary, which he made in collaboration with his friend Chris Marker, has had the most troubled career of any of his films. The shooting, which began in 1950, was interrupted and resumed only after two years, the film was banned by the censor, and finally it became the victim of a dispute among the producers. Though the film itself is unavailable one can gain an idea of the form it took from the script, published together with stills from the film by Chris Marker in his 'Commentaires' in 1961. The film was not originally intended as an indictment, as Resnais tells us: "When we set out we did not have the idea of making an anti-colonialist, anti-racialist film. It was just that we were naturally led to ask some questions, which resulted in the film being banned."[4] The pattern of the film reflects this growing awareness of where the blame for the decline of negro culture lies. The significance of the film's title is revealed in the opening words: "When men are dead they enter history. When statues are dead they enter art. This botany of death is what we call culture." The negro art of the museums is dead because it no longer receives a living, understanding glance, because it has been killed by the impact of Western civilisation. Yet the two cultures, black and white, have basically the same aims. Our science, like the art and religion of the negro, is the "instrument of a desire to seize the world." Both fight against the same enemy — death — and ultimately "there is no breach between African civilisation and ours . . . Beyond the dead forms [of negro art] we can recognise the promise, common to all great civilisations, of man as victor over the world. Whether we are black or white, our future is made of this promise." The humanism of Marker's con-

47

clusion to *Les Statues meurent aussi* is in perfect keeping with Resnais's own views. The honesty of the work is obvious — despite its left-wing sympathies this is not a work of propaganda — yet it was banned, and for over two years neither author received a proposal from a film producer. For Resnais there was the consolation of the award of the Prix Vigo in 1954 and the stimulus of work on the editing of Varda's *La Pointe Courte*. When, finally, he did resume directing in 1955 he showed that his talent had matured and he made his finest documentary.

NUIT ET BROUILLARD (1955)

This compilation film on the concentration camps was commissioned by the Comité d'Histoire de la Déportation de la Seconde Guerre Mondiale in May 1955 and finished in December of that year. Like *Les Statues meurent aussi* it won the Prix Vigo but again Resnais received little help from the authorities. As usual he chose to work in collaboration: "I did not dare to make this film myself: I was never deported myself. Then I met Jean Cayrol who had been and he agreed to make it with me. The script was partly written before we left for Poland and then modified on the spot. I did not receive anything from 'Germany except a very friendly correspondence."[2] The choice of Jean Cayrol is significant, for he is a novelist and poet whose whole conception of life and art was conditioned by his concentration camp experiences. Here in *Nuit et Brouillard* Cayrol is dealing directly with what he sees as the central experience of our age and what forms the background to all his writings. The first aim of both

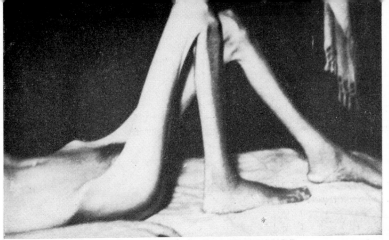

Above, an image of horror from NUIT ET BROUILLARD.

Below, Alain Resnais directing TOUTE LA MÉMOIRE DU MONDE.

TOUTE LA MÉMOIRE DU MONDE:
the prison aspect of the library.

Alain Resnais at work
LE CHANT DU STYRÈ.

writer and director was to tell the truth about the camps: not to erect yet another monument to the dead (who included Cayrol's brother Pierre, murdered in Oranienburg), but to furnish "an example on which to meditate" and offer "a summons, a warning."[42] Cayrol is concerned to testify not against a nation but against "a system which did not respect the elementary rights of everyone to his own originality and particularity." In this his attitude is very similar to that of another Christian writer, the German Protestant pastor Albrecht Goes whose Novelle 'Das Brandopfer' appeared in 1954 and begins with the reflection: "People have forgotten. And things must indeed be forgotten, for how could anyone who cannot forget live? But from time to time there must be someone there who remembers." Cayrol is such a man.

In his seriousness of purpose Cayrol is matched by his director. Resnais has his camera track through the derelict remains of Auschwitz as it is today, recording in realistic colour what is left of these places of horror. The meaning in terms of human suffering of this barbed wire and these innocent-looking buildings is made clear by the interposed black-and-white archive material — documents, photographs, newsreels — which occupies most of the film's time. The power and calm thoughtful rhythm of *Nuit et Brouillard* derive from the alternation of these two sets of images: the faded grey of the archive material contrasts with the colour of the present day shots, its immobility is set against the tracking movement of Resnais's camera, the rigidity of death opposed to the measured step of the contemporary investigator. As in his first feature, where Resnais dares to set his love story against the horrors of the atomic bomb, so here he has the audacity to make his film beautiful as well as terrible, in the belief that "if it is beautiful it can be more effective."[2] The choice of colour is particularly significant in this respect: "By making all the film in black-and-white I was afraid of obtaining from these old stones, barbed wire and leaden skies a filmic romanticism that would not have been at all genuine. The colours and the silent parts are there to show the difference. Besides in one's memory one thinks a little bit in grey, in any case in a less distinct colour."[2] The colour is used purely realistically here, as in the second film Resnais made with Cayrol, the feature *Muriel*. Eastmancolor was chosen in preference to Agfacolor because, Ghislain Cloquet tells us: "Resnais wanted a bright colour. He sought to modify, through colour, the way people habitually look at things . . . He wanted to show the sun present, because he was aiming at the present, and the future."[72]

As in most of Resnais's shorts the music has an important part to play and for this film the director had the collaboration of Hanns Eisler, the German composer and former associate of Brecht, who was driven from his homeland by the advent of Hitler. Resnais himself has explained that "the more violent the images are the gentler is the music. Eisler wanted to show that the optimism and hope of man always existed in the background."[2] Henri Colpi, who edited *Nuit et Brouillard* with his wife Jasmine Chasney, has also analysed the use of music. The film "opened with, over the credits, a long melodic phrase, ample and moving, the re-solution of which was left in suspense. This theme reappeared linking the 'before' and the 'after' of the concentration camp universe only at the very end where this time, marvellously, it is resolved. The other important motifs were the deportation theme dominated by the brass and the heartrending concentration camp theme. To contrast with the imposing staging of the Hitlerian marches, Eisler used high-pitched pizzicati. Later the pizzicati accompanied one of the results of Nazism: the huge camps, the typhus, the corpses buried by bulldozer, the SS become prisoners in their turn."[49]

Nuit et Brouillard is a highly organised work. The opening colour shots of a deceptively innocuous countryside are answered by the final ones of a crematorium black against the sky. The camera tracks forward, the commentary reminds us that even a peaceful landscape can conceal a concentration camp, and the camp as it is today is suddenly uncovered. Now it is in ruins, grass-covered and with no footstep but our own heard there, but we are reminded that it is the product of 1933 when the Nazi war machine got under way. The victims, living in blissful ignorance while the building was in progress, were eventually rounded up, transported in wagon loads of a hundred or more so that many were already dead on their arrival in night and fog. "Today on the same route there is daylight and sunshine. We walk along it slowly, searching for what? The trace of the corpses that collapsed when the doors were opened?" As we enter the camp today we are reminded of what it was once like: "a different planet". The victims stripped, humiliated, tatooed and numbered, subject to a chain of command at the head of which was the commandant, indifferent and affecting ignorance. As we walk through the camp today it is impossible for us to comprehend fully the reality of the camps, "no description, no image can give them back their true dimension, that of uninterrupted terror." As the décor of the camp is examined, the commentary and interposed shots remind us of the society that took shape behind the cynical Nazi slogans, such as 'Arbeit macht frei'.

The film does not despair — "a man is incredibly resistant" — but the efforts of the prisoners to maintain their human identity are overshadowed by the constant horror of brutality, starvation, punishment and execution. Today it is hard to find traces of the machinery of annihilation, the gas chambers and crematoria, whose work was stepped up after a visit by Himmler in 1942 — only the scratched cement of the ceilings reveals the truth to those who know where to look. In the end all that was left of these vast reservoirs of human labour were the relics of an insane attempt to make clothes and soap from human bodies and a final generation of victims incapable of understanding, even when the camps were finally opened.

Those who were in charge deny their responsibility: "Who then is to blame?" asks Cayrol and urges us to look into ourselves for the answer. "At this moment, when I am talking to you, the cold water of the marshes and ruins fills the hollow of these charnel-houses. Nature is cold and opaque like our bad memory." We must remember the millions of dead who haunt this landscape and Cayrol concludes with a warning against forgetfulness: "There are all those who did not believe it, or only from time to time. And there are

52

those of us who look sincerely at these ruins as if the old concentration camp monster were dead beneath the debris, who
pretend to take hope before this fading image, as if the concentration camp plague could be cured, who pretend to believe that all this is of one time and one country, and who do
not think to look around and who do not hear that people
cry unceasingly." It is hardly surprising that this recalls
Albert Camus's ending for 'La Peste' — "the bacillus of the
plague never dies nor disappears . . . and perhaps the day
would come when, for the misfortune and instruction of men,
the plague would awaken its rats and send them to die in a
happy city" — for in his essay 'Pour un romanesque lazaréen'
Cayrol had hailed Camus as "perhaps the first historian and
investigator of Lazarian or concentration camp art." In
Nuit et Brouillard Resnais fuses perfectly the talents of his
photographers Cloquet and Vierny, his scriptwriter Cayrol
and his composer Eisler and performs the almost impossible
task of encompassing the worst horrors of the Nazi régime
within a work of art.

TOUTE LA MÉMOIRE DU MONDE (1956)

At first sight the subject of Resnais's next film, the Bibliothèque Nationale, might seem a surprising departure for
the director. It is true that in filming there for three weeks
he satisfied an old curiosity: "For years a faithful client of the
Nationale I wanted to find out what happens between the
moment you fill in a form and the moment you receive the
book."[11] But in fact this 'sentimental walk behind the scenes'
was no more than a framework for Resnais's real interests.

53

The overall structure of the film is simple: it begins with a brief tour of the library, the camera sweeping lyrically round the dome, over the roof, along arcades, grills and stairways, past avenues of books. The various departments are visited in turn and the sheer volume of material digested by the library indicated. Then the passage of a book is followed from its arrival, through the processes of cataloguing till it reaches its place on the shelves. The treasures of the library are displayed and the methods used to preserve them explained. Then the process by which a book goes from the shelf to the reader who has requested it is shown and the film ends in the reading room where the book may function as "a fragment of a single secret, which has perhaps a very beautiful name, which is called happiness."

Toute la mémoire du monde is a film that exists on several levels. Technically this is one of Resnais's most striking films with the camera continually tracking to and fro in the maze of passages and corridors. It is not surprising to learn that the film "came out of a few bars of an operetta by Kurt Weill, 'Lady in the Dark', which gave rise to long tracking shots, separated by very brief ones, big movements that correspond as much to the baroque architecture of the Bibliothèque Nationale as to the music of Kurt Weill."[5] A perfect unison is achieved between Ghislain Cloquet's camerawork and Maurice Jarre's music, and in its hypnotic effect it anticipates the opening of *Marienbad* which Resnais made five years later. Indeed it was of this film that he thought when he came to make his first contact with Alain Robbe-Grillet's novels: "When I finished reading Robbe-Grillet's work, I said to myself: there is one film that we have clearly made together already: *Toute la mémoire du monde*."[40] On quite another level there are links with the concentration camp world of *Nuit et Brouillard*. Remo Forlani's script emphasises the prison aspect of the library: "In Paris it is in the Bibliothèque Nationale that words are imprisoned," and books are stamped "to indicate that a volume has entered the Bibliothèque Nationale, that never again will it be able to leave." Though the film was made for the French Foreign Ministry, it also contains a number of personal allusions: the list of collaborators includes Cayrol, Marker and Agnès Varda, the latter appearing briefly in a shot of the print room. Comics are not neglected: there is a credit here to Chester Gould, just as there is one to 'Fearless Fosdick' in *Le Mystère de l'Atelier Quinze*.

Within the film too there are allusions to the world of comics and science fiction, beginning with the opening shots of a mysterious looking film camera and microphone. Like the factory of *Le Chant du Styrène* the library is a dehumanised world, with people appearing as no more than shadowy silhouettes. In the list of the treasures of the Bibliothèque Nationale ("Who can say what is the most precious, most beautiful, rarest here?") are included the memoirs of Harry Dickson (Resnais's eternal science fiction project) — sandwiched between the still unpublished diaries of Romain Rolland and the manuscript of Pascal's 'Pensées'. More indicative still of the director's tastes is a shot of piles of Mandrake and Dick Tracy comics, introduced by the question: "Who can tell what will be tomorrow the truest witness of our civilisation?" This shot is all the more significant since the comics in question do not figure among the Library's six million volumes but were smuggled in by Resnais himself from his own collections. To complete this array of allusions to Resnais's stylistic sources we may note that he and Remo Forlani were, he tells us, "susceptible to a certain atmosphere, a sort of Louis Feuillade aspect which reigns in the cellars and attics of this admirable bazaar of knowledge."[11] Feuillade has always haunted Resnais's imagination and it was around this time that he conceived his projects for a version of *Fantômas* and a *Vie de Louis Feuillade*, neither of which was realised.

The obvious literary parallel for *Toute la mémoire du monde* is Jorge Luis Borges's short story 'The Library of Babel', included in the volume 'Ficciones', which begins: "The universe (which others call the Library) is composed of an indefinite, perhaps an infinite, number of hexagonal galleries, with enormous ventilation shafts in the middle, encircled by very low railings. From any hexagon the upper or lower stories are visible, interminably . . . Light comes from some spherical fruits called by the name of lamps. There are two, running transversally, in each hexagon. The light they emit is insufficient, incessant". This could almost be an extract from the script of Resnais's film which, like Borges's story, is not content with mere description. In a sense the film uses the workings of the library as a symbol for the functioning of the mind: "Forlani and I wanted to insist on this very important notion of the usefulness of books and show the infinite, vertiginous aspect of memory."[11] The very title of the film, chosen by Forlani, stresses this aspect and the work is a key one for those who wish to interpret Resnais as the 'cinéaste of memory'. The allusions are constant: "Because their memories are short, men pile up countless reminders... This gigantic memory... An exemplary memory, the Nationale stores away whatever is printed in France". The books sought by readers are "fragments of a universal memory" which pieced together are a key to happiness.

Apart from its specific qualities as a film, *Toute la mémoire du monde* also served to bring Resnais back into contact with Remo Forlani with whom he had collaborated extensively around 1948. The years 1956-7 saw several projects for feature films to be scripted by Forlani. Two described by Francis Lacassin are of particular interest. *Un Dimanche tous ensemble* (1956) no doubt attracted Resnais initially as a film on Paris, as *Ouvert pour Cause d'Inventaire* and *Toute la mémoire du monde*, in their very different ways, had been. "It was the story of a gang of adolescents who, one fine Sunday, go for a walk in Paris, from the Place de la Bastille to the Boulevard des Italiens. The project was so close to realisation that Forlani recovered advances spent without compunction. After mature reflection Resnais abandoned it for he felt incapable of directing the film in the manner anticipated: cinéma-vérité technique, camera hidden in a lorry, a great deal of improvisation."[63] A second project was for a colour film *L'Ile Noire* (1957) adapted from the adventures of Tin Tin and using stylised artificial décor and actors wearing masks designed by Hergé. This ambitious idea came to nothing, but together with *Un Dimanche tous ensemble* it gives a fascinating insight into Resnais's attitudes at this time.

There is a desire to make feature films, but not conventional ones. The possibilities offered by cinéma-vérité methods are toyed with and finally rejected in favour of a more audacious and artificial approach drawing direct inspiration from the comic strip. The tendency away from improvisation and towards stylisation is reflected in Resnais's subsequent feature work.

LE MYSTÈRE DE L'ATELIER QUINZE (1957)

A further unrealised project of Resnais and Forlani in 1957 was a series of forty 16mm films on *L'Organisation du Travail* to be produced by a mutual friend for whose production company Resnais suggested the name Protéa Films, as a tribute to the director Victorin Jasset who died in 1913. It was from this that the film *Le Mystère de l'Atelier Quinze* (1957), the least known of the documentaries with which Resnais's name is linked, evolved a few months later. Resnais's exact role in the making of this film has recently been made clear by André Heinrich, his former assistant, who actually directed the film. Heinrich writes: "Two or three weeks before the shooting Resnais asked me — I don't know why — to relieve him. By that time the script was practically finished and Resnais had already planned everything. We reviewed the problem together and made a shooting script. Resnais and his producer gave me complete freedom. In theory . . . in theory (and I am very happy about it) for the client had asked Resnais for a film and as a friend and former assistant of Resnais I owed it to myself to give 'Resnais material' to Resnais who was to edit the film himself. So, to the data we had established together, I brought modifications in the course of shooting and in turn Resnais — who was in Paris — sent me notes and suggestions for shots with a view to the editing. Resnais came on location two or three times. Luckily, because one day when I'd had an accident he himself directed a few shots. Since I was taken up again by my normal work, Resnais did the editing completely alone. I was the first to be happily surprised on seeing the result. To return to the freedom which Resnais had given me . . . Resnais makes suggestions (apart from precise notes), brings people to do exactly what he wants without imposing anything on them. That's what he did with me, and I am persuaded that he does the same thing with his scriptwriters."[62]

Le Mystère de l'Atelier Quinze, which has a commentary by Chris Marker, deals with the fight against industrial illness and focusses on the case of a workman who suddenly falls ill for no apparent reason. It is in some ways reminiscent of *Toute la mémoire du monde*. The earlier film ended with the reflection that if all the fragments of knowledge immured in the Bibliothèque Nationale could be fitted together the result might be happiness. Here the workman can only be cured by the factory doctor able to bring together the separate knowledge of the man's doctor (a stranger to the factory) the engineer (a stranger to medicine), the foreman (a stranger to the laboratory) and the chemist (a stranger to the work floor), which united together "now represented for a man the ultimate chance of recovery." This kind of subject is of course particularly appropriate to Resnais whose idea of the successful work of art is a linking of disparate elements.

LE CHANT DU STYRÈNE (1958)

Alain Resnais's last documentary was made for the Péchiney organisation, which asked him "not to explain the manufacture of polystyrene but simply to show that it was a noble material since its manufacture was very complex, demanding a great deal of knowledge, because it was entirely created by man."[5] Resnais's handling of this commission was startlingly unorthodox, frightening his sponsors at first and illustrating his taste for 'mixing sugar and salt', in the manner of Lautréamont's classic definition of Surrealism as the unexpected meeting, on a dissection table, of a sewing machine and an umbrella. On the one hand, there are the images making full use of the formal possibilities of the wide screen and the opportunities for using colour unrealistically: "In *Nuit et Brouillard* I sought only a realistic colour, as faithful a reproduction of the place as possible. In *Le Chant du Styrène*, on the contrary, there are transpositions, there are dominants which are used quite consciously."[5] Despite the terms of the commission, human beings play little part in this film, being no more than shadowy figures in a dehumanised world of pipes and machines, and the whole emphasis of the visuals is on colour, shape and pattern, making this perhaps the freest of Resnais's shorts. To contrast with this is a combination of music by Pierre Barbaud and text by Raymond Queneau, the latter one of Resnais's favourite authors. Initially Resnais wanted the text to be sung and in this respect *Le Chant du Styrène* represents the fullest expression of his lyrical tendency, as *Nuit et Brouillard* most perfectly mirrors his commitment to a humanistic philosophy.

Having reluctantly abandoned the idea of a sung commentary Resnais had to make do with a poetic text, written in alexandrines, a metrical form chosen for reasons Resnais has recorded: "This has not been understood: I was thinking of the didactic poetry of Boileau and Malherbe and it seemed to me that a text in verse would be more effective, pedagogically, and then I felt in a confused way that here was a connection between the alexandrine and cinemascope."[5] The tone of Queneau's text is set by the pun of the title and an opening that parodies Lamartine's 'Le Lac':

"O temps, suspends ton bol, ô matière plastique..."

With a verbal adroitness fully reflecting the author's double existence as encyclopaedist and humorist and impossible to capture in translation, the commentary traces the history of polystyrene from the finished object (the bowl), to the mould, to the raw material and "thus we climb back from pipe to pipe, across the desert of the pipe-work, towards the first material, towards the abstract matter." The origins of the coal and petroleum from which all derives are touched upon — "Controversial question... obscure origins..." and so in the course of some twenty minutes we have been transported from the most up-to-date of factories back to the mists of primeval time.

*   *   *

It would be difficult to over-estimate the importance for his feature film work of the ten years Resnais spent making documentaries. All the features have a precursor among the shorts: *Hiroshima mon Amour* is an expansion of the 'operatic' aspect of *Le Chant du Styrène*; *L'Année Dernière à Marienbad* a further exploration of the mental labyrinth of *Toute la mémoire du monde; Muriel* follows *Nuit et Brouillard* in recording a 'Lazarian' world where in Cayrol's words, even "those who have only known the concentration camps by hearsay begin to have the tics of this universe"; and *La Guerre est finie* spells out in contemporary terms the lesson of *Guernica*. But the real importance lies even deeper than this, for through these documentaries one can trace the shaping of Resnais's mind and the formation of his style. The words of Emmanuelle Riva in *Hiroshima:* "Looking properly is something that can, I think, be learned" are borne out by these years. Resnais's interest in ideas follows a double flow. Firstly, turning away from photographic reality to find a substitute for it in painting, he initiates a move inwards: into the enclosed world of Van Gogh's madness or the labyrinth of the Bibliothèque Nationale. But to balance this there is an outward flow, for this same concern with documents leads him back into the world by confronting him with some of the central issues of twentieth century politics: total war, colonialism, racialism. On all these issues he maintains an independence of mind which is carried over into the feature films when he comes up against the equally intractable problems of the atomic bomb, Algeria and Fascism. If *Marienbad* is the supreme example of the inward 'evasion' into the mind, it is answered by the commitment of *La Guerre est finie*.

The documentary years are equally decisive in the establishment of Resnais's visual style. It is on the editing of images that his attention is concentrated from the very start: the extraction from the paintings of Van Gogh of a story contained in them but not forming their subject; the dismantling of the spatial arrangement of Picasso's 'Guernica' and the juggling of the pieces to make a new pattern in time (much as chronological arrangement is tampered with in *Marienbad*); the opposition of filmic textures, of past and present in *Nuit et Brouillard;* the welding into a virtual symphony of a sequence of tracking shots in *Toute la mémoire du monde.* In the early films the paintings of Van Gogh, Gauguin and Picasso are broken down into a great number of tiny shots — *Van Gogh* it may be recalled contains as many as the average feature — and a new reality constructed by piecing these fragmentary images together again in a new pattern. The same method is adopted much later in Resnais's two more realistic features, *Muriel* and *La Guerre est finie*, both of which contain an abnormally large number of shots.

From *Nuit et Brouillard* to *Marienbad*, however, Resnais concentrated more on the tracking shot which, in the frequency and effectiveness of its use, became something of a stylistic trademark. It is not to be regarded as a meaningless quirk or embroidery but as a sign of Resnais's approach to his material. The camera is the eye of an investigator moving forward to see for himself, at first hand — the director sizing up his subject. Sacha Vierny, his regular director of photography, has pictured this for us: "The tracking shots, of course ... Resnais takes care of them himself ... It is a classic image to see him advancing into the set, with a view-finder in one hand and the text in the other. With one eye he frames the action, with the other he reads. As he walks he murmurs. And in this way he finds the rhythm he needs."[48] It is noteworthy that Resnais takes his camera into his sub-ject: into Picasso's painting, into Auschwitz to find traces of the past, into the library to get lost in the maze of its passages. In this he differs from a purely decorative director like Max Ophuls who uses a tracking camera to glide ele-gantly up to the façade of a building or down a flight of steps but dares not probe, as if fearing that reality is too fragile. For Resnais, on the contrary, reality is solid and tangible enough, if sometimes horrific, and his camera movement is his means of confrontation.

But for Resnais images alone do not make up a film. Perhaps because he spent several years making silent 16mm films he is keenly aware of the need for sound, and has quoted with approval A.S. Labarthe's dictum that in the cinema you can close your eyes but not your ears. He has said: "I have always attached great importance to the soundtrack. The music or text form an integral part of the image . . . I have sometimes been reproached for giving an exaggerated place to the text, but if I am to err, I prefer it to be in this direction."[4] So, to the visual rhythm of the images are added two further rhythms: a musical and a verbal one. The re-sulting synthesis of image, text and music is applied equally successfully to a prose subject like *Nuit et Brouillard* (Cloquet and Vierney — Cayrol — Eisler) and a poetic one like *Le Chant du Styrène* (Vierny — Queneau — Barbaud). It is

HIROSHIMA MON AMOUR:
the lovers (Emmanuelle Riva and Eiji Okada) at the Riverside Café.

HIROSHIMA MON AMOUR: abo
(this page) Emmanuelle Riva and I
Okada; above opposite, the ped
procession that forms part of the bad
ground; and at right the actress (Riv
at the station towards the end of the fil

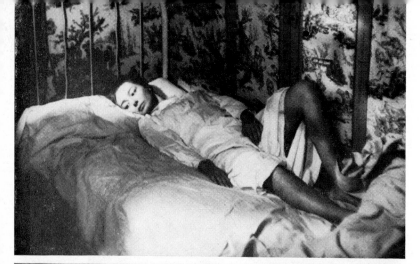

HIROSHIMA MON AMOUR. Top, the actress's memory of her madness in the cellar at Nevers. Below, the actress with her Japanese architect lover at his house (Emmanuelle Riva and Eiji Okada).

essentially a filmic conception of the cinema not in Siegfried Kracauer's sense of 'the redemption of physical reality', but in the manner conceived by Sergei Eisenstein when he wrote in 'Film Form': "The cinema would seem to be the highest stage of embodiment for the potentialities and aspirations of each of the arts."

If Resnais's reputation rested solely upon his documentary films, he would still have a high place in the history of the French cinema, but what is particularly exciting about his work is that he used his short film achievements simply as a testing ground for methods later applied to feature length subjects. It is always sad to see a film director frustrated by commercial restrictions but it is difficult to see how Resnais could have developed as he has done, if he had been able to begin a feature career as early as 1951 with an adaptation of a novel by Vailland or Queneau. Had he begun then he would surely have followed the normal patterns of film construction with their emphasis on plot and character. As it was his intellectual preoccupations were developed and his stylistic experiments carried out in the short film and when, in *Hiroshima mon Amour*, he came to include people in his films for virtually the first time, he already had, formed and fixed, structural patterns that owed nothing to the conventional film, novel or drama and were therefore to prove as revolutionary in 1959, as Orson Welles's experiments in *Citizen Kane* had appeared in 1940.

4. The Renewal of Time: Hiroshima Mon Amour

Temps jaloux, se peut-il que ces moments d'ivresse,
Où l'amour à longs flots nous verse le bonheur,
S'envolent loin de nous de la même vitesse
    Que les jours de malheur?
Hé quoi ! n'en pourrons-nous fixer au moins la trace?
Quoi ! passés pour jamais? quoi ! tout entiers perdus?
Ce temps qui les donna, ce temps qui les efface,
    Ne nous les rendra plus?
            ALPHONSE DE LAMARTINE: "Le Lac."

HIROSHIMA MON AMOUR began as a project for a documentary on the atomic bomb at which Resnais worked for five or six months with various scriptwriters without making any real progress. He merely became convinced that he was doing no more than repeating *Nuit et Brouillard* and that, in any case, the films on the bomb had already been made. But if the work on the project itself came to nothing, the act of giving it up did prove fruitful, as Resnais has explained: "So that film had come to a dead end. For my own personal pleasure I wanted to shoot 'Moderato Cantabile' in 16mm. Just as a joke, when I told the producer I was abandoning the whole affair, I added: 'Of course, if someone like Marguerite Duras were interested . . .' They took it seriously. A friend arranged for me to meet Marguerite Duras. I told her how a film on the atomic bomb itself just couldn't be made. I said to her: 'What would be pleasing would be doing a love story — in my head it was something like 'Moderato Cantabile' — but one in which the atomic agony would not be absent.' She began by saying it was indeed impossible. I also talked to her a little about the notion of characters who would not be heroes, who would not participate in the action, but would be witnesses of it, and what we are in most cases when we are confronted with catastrophes or great problems: spectators."[21] It was from this conversation that *Hiroshima mon Amour* was born. The terms of the co-production agreement with the Daiei Motion Picture Company left Resnais with virtually a free hand, for the Japanese merely stipulated a film in two episodes, one set in France and one in Japan, and two stars, one from each country. From the very first the collaboration with Marguerite Duras promised much, for Resnais had long been a fervent admirer of her novels, while she knew and admired *Nuit et Brouillard* and was willing to comply with all the director's wishes with regard to the elaboration of the script.

The basic pattern of *Hiroshima mon Amour* was Resnais's: "I brought Marguerite Duras only a vague idea of construction, simply the plan of a love story which takes place in Hiroshima and evokes, by means of parallel montage, an event which happened in 1944, during the war. If you like, I just gave Marguerite Duras something purely abstract."[21] Within this framework Duras elaborated her story, encouraged by Resnais to keep to her own personal style, just as if she were writing a novel. He intended from the first to use her work as a kind of libretto which he could 'set to images': "I intended to compose a sort of poem in which the images would act as counterpoint to the text,"[3] and: "The film links up with my preoccupation with 'making an opera'."[6] The writing took just nine weeks — far less than

67

any other Resnais film — and set the trend to be followed in the subsequent films: the director himself writing absolutely nothing but keeping in constant touch with Marguerite Duras and the 'literary adviser', Gérard Jarlot. As Duras herself said: "We saw each other every day, and every day Resnais told me where he had got to and whether or not the development of the story suited him."[53] In the preface to the Gallimard edition of the script she regretted that she could not record "the almost daily conversation between Resnais and myself, Gérard Jarlot and myself, and all three of us together. Their advice was always precious and I was never able to begin work on any episode without submitting the previous one to them and listening to their comments, which were always lucid, demanding and productive."[88] Resnais asked her to supplement the script with complete biographies of the characters, so that he knew all about them, "their youth, their existence before the film and also, to a certain extent, their future after the film."[53]

Since Marguerite Duras was encouraged to be faithful to her literary concerns, *Hiroshima mon Amour* naturally has many affinities with the world of her fiction. Like so many of her novels (including 'The Afternoon of Monsieur Andesmas' and '10.30 on a Summer Night') it reveals a feminine sensibility and concentrates on two or three characters and a limited time-span. The external event is a chance meeting (as in 'The Square'), the birth of a relationship, the growth of which may be stunted by circumstances but which, through the thoughts and dialogue it provokes, lays bare a whole lifetime of doubts and hopes, memories and illusions. Identical motifs occur in the film and the novels. Monsieur Andesmas is, in his way, as haunted by memory as the actress heroine of *Hiroshima:* "He suddenly recalled the smell of Valérie's hair when she was a child and his eyes closed with suffering at the thought of such impotence, the last in his life," or again: "The graceful memory of his old suffering hardly stirred within him, hardly more than the memory of the inconsolable regret for a love barely glimpsed, and immediately stifled, and with thousands of others, forgotten." The anonymous heroine of 'The Square' anticipates an experience like that of the film's heroine at Hiroshima: "I understand you, I really do, but you must also try to understand me. Even if the most important part of my life is over, I can't know it as yet and I haven't the time to understand it. I hope one day I will know, as you did with your journey, and that when I look back everything behind me will be clear and fall into place." '10.30 on a Summer Night' even provides a commentary on one of the episodes towards the end of *Hiroshima:* "Claire knew he was following her. She knew. He had already done so. He knew how to follow a woman he desired, from just the right distance so that she would become a little more tense than necessary. He preferred them like that."

Resnais shot the major part of *Hiroshima mon Amour* in August and September 1958 in Japan, the exteriors at Hiroshima and the interiors at Tokyo. Under the terms of the contract he was allowed to take only one technician with him and it is indicative of his concern with detail that he chose Sylvette Baudrot, the continuity girl, who also doubled as assistant and stand-in. Resnais had never been to the East before (though Marguerite Duras, being born in Vietnam, knew something of Oriental life) and before the shooting began his first act was to assure himself that the locations would fit the script he had brought with him. He spent several nights wandering the streets of Hiroshima with his Leica to capture the atmosphere and to see the city as his heroine sees it. The script itself was strictly adhered to: "I changed practically nothing in Duras's text from the moment I arrived there. Besides there was no way of doing it. We exchanged a few letters, I asked for certain replies, but the mail didn't arrive. It took six or seven days for a letter to be sent and a reply received."[21] There were certain language difficulties with the all-Japanese crew and with Eiji Okada who spoke no French, but Jean Cocteau's *Orphée* served as a "very precious system of references"[6] for Resnais, who could use it to explain his intentions to the Japanese director of photography. On his return from Japan and before he began shooting the Nevers sections of the film in December 1958, Resnais asked Duras to describe the French provincial town as the heroine would see it from Japan. The annotations of still non-existent images (published as 'Nocturnal Notes' in an appendix to the script) guided him and Sacha Vierny in their work of completing the film.

Resnais shot the major part of *Hiroshima* in August and September 1958 in Japan, the exteriors at Hiroshima and the interiors at Tokyo. Under the terms of the contract he was allowed to have only one technician with him

*   *   *

Hiroshima mon Amour has a marked dramatic structure, with the action falling into five distinct acts. The first, the

70

prologue, comprises two parts. Firstly there are the opening shots of two embracing bodies "as if drenched with ashes, rain, dew or sweat" which form a poetic image, linking the ideas of love and death, pleasure and pain. The petrified bodies here, perhaps subconsciously inspired in Duras by a novel on Pompeii she had been reading, are paralleled by a later reference to iron being "made as vulnerable as flesh" by the atomic explosion. From these formless, anonymous shapes, the bodies of the lovers emerge, but initially the tone remains unreal, since the ensuing dialogue is incantatory and described by Resnais as "a sort of dream, a voice coming from the unconscious, which is at one and the same time that of the authors and that of the spectators, which will only later become that of the principal characters. It is a kind of great advancing tracking shot into the clouds of the unconscious to reach the two characters, a way of painting a sensory atmosphere which perhaps allows us, afterwards, to give this love story a new resonance."[21] As the woman's voice enumerates what she has seen and we see documentary shots of the aftermath of the disaster, a man's voice reiterates: "You saw nothing in Hiroshima, nothing." To visit museums, to understand intellectually is not to grasp the essence of the catastrophe that Hiroshima represents. Together these two hypnotic sequences capture the mood of the whole film: the setting is revealed to us in what is, in effect, a documentary on the impossibility of comprehending, the central themes of memory and forgetfulness, love and death, mutilation by the bomb and deformation by love are stated, and the structural pattern of the film is made apparent in the verbal and musical repetitions. The prologue ends when, from this allegorical and impersonal exchange, the film moves on to real bodies in a real bed.

The film's second section — Night and Morning — is in this new realistic vein and shows the lovers getting to know each other after their night of love-making, and then separating inconclusively. At dawn the woman is reminded of an earlier lover by the movement of the sleeping man's hand but the full significance of the totally unexpected four-second thought flash is not revealed at this stage. Instead we stay in the present and see the man bring her to talk of Nevers where she spent her childhood and where she was once mad. An air of mystery persists, although we learn a good deal about the lovers — she is an actress, with a husband and children in Paris, who has come to Hiroshima to play a nurse in a film on peace, and the Japanese, likewise married, is an architect interested in politics. Yet we never learn their names and this throws into relief the two names which do return again and again in their conversation: Nevers and Hiroshima.

The third part of the film — Day — repeats the movement from documentary to personal story. It begins with shots of a peace procession: marching men, women and children, anti-nuclear banners and placards, accompanied by Japanese music. Here on the film-set the lovers meet again and, filled with desire, he takes her back to his house. There they make love and as they lie together afterwards her memories start to flow as she remembers her wartime German soldier lover. These recollections are prompted by the Japanese who has chosen Nevers as his means of comprehending her. We

72

see shots of Nevers as she recalls it and images conveying the joy of first love. But the present reasserts itself and she admits to her Japanese lover that she has only sixteen hours before she leaves Hiroshima for ever.

Night shots of Hiroshima lead into the fourth sequence set in the Riverside Café where the lovers sit together. Firstly she talks in a general way about Nevers and the Loire and we see the appropriate documentary-style images. The whole pattern of the subsequent part of the film is determined by the recurrent, alternating tracking shots of Nevers and Hiroshima, running side by side as she moves from past to present and back again. The power of memory is so strong that her German and Japanese lovers are fused into one as she becomes dominated by thoughts of blood and death, shame and suffering. This wave of recollection dies away, only to be stirred afresh by a juke box record. The cellar at Nevers where she was locked up, the shaving of her head, her madness and recovery all come back to her, but she is horrified by her own ability to forget: "Oh! It's horrible. I'm beginning to remember you less clearly. I'm beginning to forget you. I tremble at the thought of having forgotten so much love." She is driven to hysteria when she recalls her German lover's death and the hours she spent with his dead body finding only similarities between him and herself. The Japanese slaps her face to bring her back to normal and, more calmly, she completes the story of her recovery, of leaving Nevers for Paris to arrive there on the day that news of Hiroshima appeared in the newspapers. Now she emerges from the past to face the fact that this present love too is doomed to oblivion. It is late, the bar closes and the lovers again make inconclusive farewells as she returns to her hotel.

The film ends with a long decrescendo. Alone in her room she comes to terms with what has happened: "I told our story. I was unfaithful to you tonight with this stranger. I told our story. It was, you see, a story that could be told." Driven out of the hotel by her restlessness, she meets her Japanese lover again, decides mentally to stay; but he fails to make the necessary gesture as they walk the streets one behind the other. They wander to the station, then to a night club where another Japanese attempts to pick her up in a grotesque parody of their meeting twenty-four hours before. She now faces up to the nature of forgetfulness and to her own great passion being "une histoire de quatre sous." But the lovers cannot bring themselves to part and the film ends with them together in her room, "looking at each other without seeing each other", and repeating their names: "Hi-ro-shi-ma. Hi-ro-shi-ma. That's your name ... Your name is Nevers. Ne-vers in France."

* * *

Hiroshima mon Amour came after ten years' work in the documentary field and began as a project for a film on the atomic bomb so it is perhaps appropriate to begin by looking at its documentary aspects. These are clearly used to counterpoint the personal story, heralding a fresh stage of recollection and becoming less pronounced as the memory grows stronger. Each time a distancing effect is brought to bear and the film contains no direct propaganda though it takes political issues seriously. Nevers is evoked not as an indictment of occupation and liberation, but as it might appear, fourteen years later, from the other side of the world. The case against the bomb is put in the form of a film within a film and since we are shown the organisation and contrivance of the peace rally scenes, Resnais avoids all trace of emotive pleading. A note by Duras in her script is of interest in this respect: "We gather that they have just finished shooting an enlightening film on peace at Hiroshima. It's not necessarily a ridiculous film, merely an enlightening one ... Except for a few children, no one looks, they are used to seeing films being shot at Hiroshima." Similarly the opening allegorical exchange is a documentary on the inability to comprehend, not a 'film with a message'. The characters in *Hiroshima* do not participate directly in the great events evoked but the documentary material does add weight to the two *leitmotifs* of the film, the names Hiroshima and Nevers. The love story gains by being set against a backcloth of death but as Duras's script tells us: "This personal story always dominates the necessarily demonstrative Hiroshima story." The characters of the film were conceived as people with political beliefs but these are left implicit: the German is not shown to be an anti-Nazi and the simple phrase 'Je fais de la politique' is all there is to convey the Japanese's left-wing commitment (though it is notable that both Duras and Resnais have said they find these words unambiguous). Resnais in fact keeps to the artistic credo of all his films up to *La Guerre est finie:* "I have no message. I try above all to react personally and simply to a subject. I try to adopt a definite position regarding an event, a story, a point, that is all. The rest is only journalism."[18]

Hiroshima mon Amour also follows naturally on the documentaries in the structural patterns it adopts, for Resnais's great achievement is to maintain in a feature the short film maker's freedom to build a film out of an interplay of past and present (as in *Nuit et Brouillard*) or by the systematic use of successive tracking shots (as in *Toute la mémoire du monde*). His conception of the cinema as a combination of visual and aural rhythms in which the editor's role in juxtaposing the elements is a prime creative function is fully sustained in *Hiroshima* which is built around a series of contrasts and incongruities. These latter — text and images, documentary and personal story, past and present, destruction and love, Hiroshima and Nevers — are, however, never simply equated. To take one example, Resnais rightly said of the last of these: "We oppose the immense, fantastic, enormous side of Hiroshima and the tiny little story of Nevers which is reflected to us through it, as the light of a candle is reflected, enlarged and inverted by a lens."[6] The film's structure bears this out: the Nevers episodes, which were shot last, are fitted into the Hiroshima framework in three successive phases: the initial flash shot, the balance of two moments of intense joy and finally the anguish of death out-weighing the sorrow of parting. But though as it is told Nevers overwhelms Hiroshima so that the Japanese is seen as no more than an extension of the German (as he says at the beginning of the Riverside Café scene: "When you are in the cellar, am I dead?"), the mere verbalisation destroys its magic, and by the end of the film the Japanese protagonist has recovered his identity: "Hi-ro-shi-ma, Hi-ro-shi-ma. That's your name." The weighting of the two episodes is also reflected in the way the Nevers scenes are always shown to the accompaniment of Japanese sounds, except in the single (and therefore enormously powerful) moment of the heroine's scream. This maintenance of a tension between what is seen and what is heard occurs throughout the film. At the beginning, the heroine's voice talks of Hiroshima, fifteen days after the explosion, as being blanketed with flowers but what we see on the screen is a child's blinded eye manipulated with surgical instruments, while at the end, during the night walk through the streets of the town, we hear the heroine's thoughts: "He's going to come towards me, he's going to take me by the shoulders, he's going to kiss me ... He'll kiss me ... and I'll be lost", but we see that in fact he is dropping back as if discouraged. In a similar way Resnais often derives impact from dual associations within a single image — as in the opening shot with its ideas of skin as the source both of pleasure and of pain[6] — or, more frequently still, within a single speech: "You destroy me. You're so good for me" or "I lie. And I tell the truth."

Basing his film on this kind of recurrent dichotomy rather than on traditional narrative preconceptions Resnais gives it a structural pattern that follows an essentially musical form. He realised the risks of disconcerting or boring the spectators involved in this but his desire for innovation proved stronger. This is shown most distinctly in the opening and closing of

77

the film. In place of a clear-cut exposition we find a desire "to provoke a kind of uneasiness in the first quarter of an hour that would correspond a little to that of a dream or nightmare",[21] and where a vivid climax might be expected comes a slow running-down of the relationship, with eight or nine pairs of parallel tracking shots of Nevers and Hiroshima and the heroine communing only with herself. Resnais himself chose a musical analogy by which to define his film. He said: "I know nothing about musical composition but if it implies having a theme and building variations and counterpoints then this is quite true. I think that if you analysed *Hiroshima* with a diagram on graph paper you would witness something close to a quartet. Themes, variations on the first movement, from these repetitions and flashbacks which some people find insufferable and which besides may well be so for those who do not enter into the game. The last movement of the film is a slow movement, a decrescendo."[6] Like a piece of music *Hiroshima mon Amour* depends entirely on its rhythmical structure and Resnais has recorded that the shortened version made at the instance of the producers seemed "much longer than before, almost imcomprehensible, bizarre, gratuitous and in any case no less boring."[5] The adherence to this revolutionary pattern took a great deal of courage, and during the shooting the director was assailed by doubts. He made Marguerite Duras describe fully every Nevers scene before he shot it and contemplated padding out these sequences with more narrative: "I therefore accentuated the anecdotal side of certain scenes but I finally noticed that this did not fit in with the film. So at the editing stage I cut everything that depended on anecdote, which incidentally, implies a great respect for the audience."[6]

In the triple mixture of elements that go to make up *Hiroshima mon Amour* music plays a vital role. Resnais has often stressed the importance this has for him and once went so far as to say that he could not conceive of a film without music.[21] His attitude to composing is in marked contrast to his attitude towards writing a film: "I'm not musical, I don't know how to write a score, but I should very much like to, if I could."[21] The music of *Hiroshima*, perhaps the most successful of all Resnais's film scores, is largely the work of Giovanni Fusco, Antonioni's habitual composer. Georges Delerue, whose name also appears in the credits, contributed only the wonderfully evocative waltz tune played on the juke box in the Riverside Café scene, and all the rest — apart from a few minutes of authentic Japanese music — is Fusco's. Resnais had a certain initial reluctance about contacting Fusco but in the event the meeting of composer and director was instantly and startlingly successful: "It sounds like a fairy tale. Fusco arrived in Paris within twenty-four hours. At midday I was showing him the working copy of *Hiroshima* and by seven in the evening he was explaining the film to me. He had felt and assimilated it totally. He had understood everything: the game of contradictions, of oblivion ... everything. In just one day we came to an agreement about the music. Perhaps you can remember Hanns Eisler's music for *Nuit et Brouillard*? Well, what is extraordinary is that in *Hiroshima* — at the beginning for the museum sequence — there is a melodic phrase which for twenty seconds is abso-

79

lutely Eisler's theme, which Fusco was totally unacquainted with and which he had spontaneously rediscovered."[6] The music, written for a combination of piano, flute, piccolo, clarinet, saxophone, 'cello, doublebass, horn and guitar and accompanying virtually the whole film, consists of a number of distinct themes. Henri Colpi, who edited the film, has shown in his invaluable analysis of the score[49] how these interweave: the 'oblivion' theme (Oubli) providing as it were a framework for those associated with physical love (Corps), the joy of first romance (Nevers) and the plenitude of love (Fleuve). These themes are, moreover, never linked to a single image or character but rather follow the state of mind of the characters and the flow of their feelings.

The images show the same concern with rhythm and counterpoint as the music. Most striking is the use of the tracking shots and Resnais drew on the formal researches undertaken in his last short films to achieve a balance and interaction of Nevers and Hiroshima, past and present, by means of pairs of tracking shots moving at the same speed and placed side by side. For the maintenance of this equilibrium Resnais consciously set out to obtain contrasting sets of images. Not only did he use different makes of film stock and different directors of photography for the two halves (Michio Takahashi for Hiroshima and Sacha Vierny for Nevers), he also refused to let Vierny see the material that had been shot in Japan so that he could not possibly be influenced by it, even subconsciously. The Nevers episodes have a tone of their own not merely because of the softer light of the Loire valley in winter but also thanks to the use of lenses

L'ANNÉE DERNIÈRE À MARIENBAD: one of the
'false' dénouements — the rape of the heroine (*Delphine Seyrig*).

Delphine Seyrig in L'ANNÉE DERNIÈRE À MARIENBAD. "*We can imagine* MARIENBAD *is a documentary on a statue*" *(Alain Robbe-Grillet)*.

with a long focal length which both give the impression of bringing people and settings forward to meet the spectator and slow down the movement of the characters to a dream-like pace. The combination of these shots and the gay and lively Nevers theme gives these sequences of joyful first love an air that anticipates Truffaut's *Jules et Jim*, while the earlier and more solemn tracking shots through the hospital at Hiroshima, linked so expertly to the newsreel shots, show Resnais at his unique documentary best.

Set against music and images is Marguerite Duras's text, the tone of which is perhaps best defined as one of lyrical detachment: there is a surrender to feeling and emotion which permeates all the film and is allowed to dictate its shape and yet at the same time a lucid awareness of the corrosive effect of time and of the fourteen years that separate Nevers and Hiroshima. Resnais had already employed poetical texts in his shorts, working with Paul Eluard on *Guernica* and Raymond Queneau in *Le Chant du Styrène*, and in this first feature he embarks on a programme he had set himself: "I would like above all to react against the traditional theatrical structures, against the tone of the so-called psychological drama. What I should like is to recover a certain lyrical tone, that is to say, in fact, to end up with opera."[6] Frequently the text is used in ways that are very effective though totally undramatic in a conventional sense. There is for example the passage accompanied by shots of the river and the first statement of the 'Fleuve' theme (used to signify the plenitude of love): "The seven branches of the delta estuary in the Ota river drain and fill at the usual hour, exactly at the usual hours, with water that is fresh and rich with fish, grey or blue depending on the hour or the season. Along the muddy banks people no longer watch the tide rising slowly in the seven branches of the delta estuary of the river Ota." The use of repetition is even more marked in the scene at the Japanese's house when Resnais, instead of choosing what he felt to be the most vivid and dramatic of Duras's three suggested dialogue possibilities, instead employed them all: "It was there, I seem to have understood, that you were so young . . . so young you still don't belong to anyone in particular. — It was there, I seem to have understood, that I almost . . . lost you . . . and that I risked never knowing you. — It was there, I seem to have understood, that you must have begun to be what you are today." In giving more weight to this lyrical tone than to plot development Resnais also makes largely irrelevant the conventional concept of character, for such a use of language has the effect of diverting the spectator's attention from individual idiosyncrasies to the flow of emotion, thereby preventing the normal identification with the protagonists to which we are accustomed in the cinema.

The fostering of this detachment on the part of the spectator is an avowed part of Resnais's basic approach to the film medium: "If I made the films I dream of making, it would be less to destroy or demolish than to provoke the spectator to question his own assumptions. My aim is to put the spectator in such a state that a week, six months or a year afterwards, placed before a problem, he would be prevented from cheating and obliged to react freely."[4] The key concept here, that of freedom, obviously has similarities with Brecht's preoccupations in the theatre but it also ties up with Resnais's literary tastes and perhaps helps to explain why he has always turned to novelists for his scripts. The modern novelist, as Resnais sees him, approaches his characters in such a way as to "show their acts in a raw state, such as they appear to him spontaneously as he writes. It is a way of provoking the reader by inviting him to justify these acts for himself."[38] Elsewhere he has spoken of his desire "to leave the spectator as much freedom of imagination as the reader of a novel has", and expressed the hope that "around the image, behind the image and even within the image, he can give his imagination free rein, while at the same time submitting to the screen's fascination."[4]

We have already seen how free from bias and propaganda the documentary sections of *Hiroshima* are, and it is clear that the same attitude is adopted in the presentation of people. Resnais does not say 'This is what the woman is like', he merely shows her to us and allows us to draw our own conclusions. Wide and important as the issues tackled in the short films had been, human beings are more complex still and give *Hiroshima* a richness that the rather abstract documentaries lacked. Resnais is deeply concerned with matters of form and style but only in so far as these allow him to present characters in their full complexity. For Resnais working with actors — professional ones, not amateurs picked out in the streets — is an essential part of film-making. Emmanuelle Riva was an experienced actress in the theatre when Resnais met her and it is indicative of the gulf which separates him from Rossellini and the neo-realist concept of film acting, that he chose her as much for the quality of her voice as for her physical appearance. He needed a talented, fully professional actress capable not simply of giving the realistic portrayal of a French married woman having a brief affair in Japan, but also of capturing the non-naturalistic tone of the opening dialogue and conveying the flow of emotion in any given scene. Character as Resnais sees it does not provide a simple prop for the actor: "For me the ideal character is one who in three speeches becomes attractive, then in three more repellent. It is between these two poles that you can try to grasp the ambiguity of life. You cannot make definitive judgments, everything is constantly questioned."[4] The heroine of *Hiroshima mon Amour* is a fine example of this notion and Resnais's own attitude towards her is interesting: "Take me, for example, how that girl can get me annoyed sometimes! You just cannot imagine! Sometimes she behaves like such a . . . It's just that after being awake for twenty-four hours, you end up doing silly things. Especially in the conditions in which she has been living: as well as the lack of sleep there is the fatigue of walking and the drink. Walking in the town for example, that's a silly thing to do."[6] It is this personal reaction that Resnais succeeds so well in conveying.

The characters are not naturalistically observed human beings — there are moments, especially at the beginning and end, when they cease to be 'real' people at all — but they come alive because they provoke the same mixture of sympathy and antagonism as the people we meet day by day. They are not in any way heroic, and if great events form a background to the story, the characters nonetheless remain apart from them: the actress experienced love, not the occupation, at Nevers and neither is directly connected with the disaster of Hiroshima. They hardly remember or recollect it in any meaningful way and in so far as the city is important it is as a further element of counterpoint: a background of death for a story of love: "For Hiroshima too there was no question of raising a monument to the dead. There more than elsewhere living is what matters. Everywhere you feel the presence of death. As a reaction you feel a violent appetite for life, a desire for immediate sensations. That is a banal psychological reality, and may perhaps explain a certain need for sexual freedom."[4] The characters are also in no way idealised, they are not presented as exemplary types or as particularly enviable human beings. The passion they experience is one of the great moments of their lives but their encounter began as a sexual adventure and both will be drawn back to their married life afterwards. This at least is the way in which the film was originally conceived, but an ambiguity remains since the characters are not totally defined. The German for instance is real enough but we know nothing of him, not even his name, so that he remains in a sense a blank for us to fill in, a face for us to interpret, while the end of the film is left deliberately open. It is interesting to note that the more Resnais talked to interviewers, the less certain he became about the lovers' separation. Whereas in July 1959 he replied to a question about whether the woman stays with the words: "For myself I do not think she can. You do not live what she has lived and at that intensity, without a break occurring very quickly"[6], by February 1960 he felt that the affair might last a fortnight longer.[7]

*　　*　　*

Hiroshima mon Amour does not need a strong dramatic ending because its reliance on plot is minimal. It has no story to tell in the normal sense: nothing is finalised between the lovers, the film beginning after they have decided to sleep together and ending before they decide whether or not to separate. Instead there is a reliance, as has been seen, on the rhythms of words, music and images, a bringing together of the two great love experiences of a woman's life to show the interplay between them. In these two far from exemplary love affairs the essential of her life is revealed: a struggle against the constrictions first of a provincial adolescence, then of a conventional marriage. Each time she hears words of love spoken to her in a foreign accent and this perhaps, as much as anything, causes the second love to revive the first. It is in its handling of time that *Hiroshima mon Amour* proves its total originality, being a film that owes nothing to the conventions of narrative of other art forms but uses simply the cinema's ability to fuse past and present into a continuous flow. The stories of Nevers and Hiroshima develop simultaneously and with the heroine we move constantly from one to the other as they illuminate each other across the gulf of fourteen years. In this way the cinema's unique ability to capture more realistically than any other art form the non-chronological ebb and flow of our mental processes becomes more evident than ever before. If the sound film may be said to have regained its awareness of cinematic space, freeing itself from the tyranny of the studio set, with *Paisa* and the Italian neo-realists, so here, in *Hiroshima mon Amour*, perhaps for the first time a film explored the full possibilities of cinematic time.

5. In the Labyrinth:
L'Année Dernière à Marienbad

*The explanation is obvious. "The Garden of Forking Paths"
is a picture, incomplete yet not false, of the universe such as
Ts'ui Pên conceived it to be ... He believed in an infinite
series of times, in a dizzily growing, ever spreading network
of diverging, converging and parallel times. This web of time
— the strands of which approach one another, bifurcate,
intersect or ignore each other through the centuries — em-
braces every possibility.*

JORGE LUIS BORGES: "Ficciones".

*Everything leads us to believe that there exists a spot in the
mind from which life and death, the real and the imaginary,
the past and the future, the high and the low, the communi-
cable and the incommunicable will cease to appear contradictory.*

ANDRÉ BRETON: "Second Surrealist Manifesto".

AFTER *Hiroshima mon Amour* Resnais considered a
number of widely divergent projects more or less simultaneously, a practice he has continued throughout the
sixties. Firstly there were the ones that followed logically
from such short films as *Nuit et Brouillard* and *Guernica* and
the documentary aspects of *Hiroshima mon Amour* by confronting the social and political issues of contemporary
French society, in particular the Algerian question. In this
vein he contemplated an adaptation of Daniel Anselme's
novel 'La Permission', which was soon abandoned because
he felt that it would have been very difficult to capture the
work's sociologically realistic tone.[5] He also worked for some
time with Anne-Marie de Villaine on a script for a film to
be called *A suivre à n'en plus finir*, dealing with the reper-

cussions of the Algerian War on a young married couple when the husband is recalled to military service, but this project too came to nothing. A further script dealing with everyday life, Jean Cayrol's *Muriel*, did materialise, but only as Resnais's third feature, after a film of a very different kind, *L'Année Dernière à Marienbad*. This latter represents a totally different line of approach, which fascinated Resnais equally at this time and likewise had its roots in his short films and its clearest expression so far in *Hiroshima mon Amour*, namely the idea of probing deeply into the mental processes of a character. This film would be "non-chronological, a film where the vision would change each moment, where the décor, the situation would be completely modified in the course of the same scene." Some of his comments in 1960 on *Hiroshima* show the way his thoughts were moving. In Japan, he tells us, the film-makers used to sit around in the evenings telling stories about the heroine: "she is a mythomaniac and the story of Nevers which she relates to her Japanese has never taken place"[5] or again: "she is not in Hiroshima but in an asylum and she is the one who invents all this adventure."[5] Resnais met Roger Vailland, whose early novels had made such an impact on him, to discuss a film on these lines, but nothing came of the meeting. Then, in 1960, he came into contact with Alain Robbe-Grillet.

Despite the often alleged links between Alain Resnais and the 'nouveau roman' he had not read any of Robbe-Grillet's work when the suggestion of collaboration was first made. By 1960 Robbe-Grillet had established a reputation as an important, if controversial, novelist with four books already published: 'Les Gommes' (1953), 'Le Voyeur' (1955), 'La Jalousie' (1957) and 'Dans le Labyrinthe' (1959). He was strongly attracted to the cinema and the possibility of film-making for various reasons, including one that brought him close to Resnais, i.e. "the possibility of presenting with every appearance of unquestionable objectivity, what, moreover, is only dream or memory; in a word, what is only imagination."[80] It was this which was to be the basis of *Marienbad* and also of Robbe-Grillet's own first two films as director: *L'Immortelle* (1963), which he was preparing in Turkey while Resnais was shooting *Marienbad*, and *Trans-Europ-Express* (1967).

The initiative for *L'Année Dernière à Marienbad* came from the producers Raymond Froment and Pierre Courau who brought Resnais and Robbe-Grillet together in the winter of 1959-60. The writer was well disposed towards the prospect of working with Resnais since he was familiar with his work, admired it and recognised parallels to his own efforts both in style and subject-matter. Stylistically he appreciated "a somewhat ritual deliberation, a certain slowness, a sense of the theatrical, even that occasional rigidity of attitude, that hieratic quality in gesture, word and setting which suggests both a statue and an opera."[90] As far as subject-matter was concerned he could detect "an attempt to construct a purely mental space and time — those of dreams, perhaps, or of memory, those of any effective life — without excessive insistence on the traditional relations of cause and effect, nor on an absolute time-sequence in narrative."[90] The meeting of the two men was a complete success and they found themselves in total agreement as to what they wanted to do. They discussed not 'subjects' but 'cinematic forms'. They wondered, Robbe-Grillet tells us, "if it would be possible to extend the 'flash-back' or hypothesis system, so frequent in detective films, to a generalisation of the mental image, that is to say an image presented as realistic but in fact representing either what is happening inside a person or between two people."[38] They also agreed that their film should be addressed "directly to the spectator's sensibility, rather than to his spirit of analy-sis."[39] A week after this meeting took place Robbe-Grillet presented Resnais with four script projects of about a page and a half each, and the two of them agreed on one — the most 'austere' according to Resnais — which subsequently became *L'Année Dernière à Marienbad*.

*   *   *

Of all his feature films, this is the one to which Resnais contributed least in the scripting stage. Robbe-Grillet wrote it in its entirety, providing a shot by shot description of the film as he imagined it, including camera movement, sounds, music and dialogue. Resnais in fact made his shooting script in about two and a half days and had for a time the feeling that his part was no more than that of an 'electronic robot'[8]. Robbe-Grillet worked essentially on his own during the writing and the second major discussion (and agreement) with Resnais came only after the script was finished. Resnais made regular visits to follow the progress of the scenario, but most of his suggestions for broadening or altering the film clashed with the form it seemed to be acquiring spontaneously: "There was a time during the preparation of *Marienbad* when I would arrive with my little black note-book and propose to Robbe-Grillet, for example, making the real world intervene in the form of conversations about a political problem that seemed insoluble, at least to those having the conversations. But we realised that it was the spectators themselves who, when they saw the film, would naturally represent the real world and that it was therefore impossible to include them in advance inside the film. I had also wanted the woman to be pregnant at one time, but it was hardly possible. We were not free. Besides, I'm of the opinion that you do not make the films you want to."[9]

The unpleasant sense of being a prisoner of someone else's ideas was dissipated for Resnais as soon as shooting began, for he then found himself, seemingly miraculously, right in the middle of his own favourite world: "I remember the first shot we saw the rushes of. It was the shot of the young woman, in full sunshine, on the balustrade behind the statue. When the lights went on again, I said to myself: that's funny, we are right in the middle of the film serials of Feuillade."[40] The feeling of being bound to a pre-existing form did, however, persist for Resnais and all the crew during the shooting and at the editing stage when he and Henri Colpi, who had expected to be completely free in editing a non-chronological film, ended up with a film which corresponded almost exactly to the initial plan. Robbe-Grillet had no connection with the film between the completion of the script and the final stage of editing, and his reaction to what he saw then is one of the finest of tributes Resnais has received from his writers and as good a summary as one could ever hope to make of the particular contribution of a *metteur en scène* to his films: "I did not think it would be so beautiful. I recognised it completely, of course, but at the same time it had become marvellous. Basically everything was foreseen and everything remained to be done."[40]

* * *

The impossibility of giving an adequate synopsis of *L'Année Dernière à Marienbad*, makes it virtually unique among feature films. The categories of 'plot' and 'character' no longer have any meaning and to express the film in such terms is to give an interpretation that both limits and distorts it. Perhaps a better introduction is to consider the elements of the film in turn. Alain Robbe-Grillet, in his introduction to the published script, describes the action in these terms: "The whole film, as a matter of fact, is the story of a *persuading:* it deals with a reality which the hero creates out of his own vision, out of his own words. And if his persistence, his secret conviction, finally prevail, they do so among a perfect labyrinth of false trails, variants, failures and repetitions!"[90] The setting is an enormous baroque hotel, with innumerable rooms and endless corridors all filled with a wealth of decoration: pillars, mouldings, gilded ornaments. Outside there are only formal gardens, statues, fountains, with nowhere a trace of untamed nature, and indeed the whole setting forms a world totally cut off from reality, hermetically sealed against social, political or economic pressures. Within this stifling world moves a rich, anonymous clientèle, occupied with worldly pursuits: dancing, cards, dominoes, pistol-shooting and polite conversation. In the foreground are three people, nameless in the film but designated by the letters A, X and M in the script. X is the stranger, the outsider, who approaches A and attempts to convince her that they met last year, fell in love and agreed to wait a year before running off together. A does not remember, or feigns forgetfulness, and clings to the calm, ordered life offered her by M who is perhaps her husband. But X insists and the pattern of *L'Année Dernière à Marienbad* is largely conditioned by her responses: amusement, growing anxiety, terror, submission. In the end A and X do leave together but only to enter a fresh labyrinth.

However we are to approach this film certain initial assumptions have to be made and Robbe-Grillet in his essay 'Time and Description in Contemporary Narrative' puts forward two that allow immediate access to the film. Firstly, the images of the film depict mental life, not outer reality as it is normally recorded by the camera: "We can only be dealing here with a subjective, mental, personal development. These things must be happening in someone's mind."[80] Exactly whose mind they are happening in is questionable, but it can readily be accepted that the images are mental ones, since they follow no normal chronological or logical sequence but rather the para-logic of a dream. The second premise is perhaps less easily grasped or appreciated. Despite Resnais's reputation as the 'cinéaste of memory' and despite the title 'Last Year', the film has nothing to do with the past or forgetfulness. To quote Robbe-Grillet again: "The universe in which the film takes place is, characteristically, that of a perpetual present which makes any recourse to memory impossible."[80] This is a proposition that will require justification and explanation but it in fact represents the key to the whole film, the thread by means of which the labyrinth of *Marienbad* can be mastered.

L'Année Dernière à Marienbad is a realistic film, as Resnais has said, but it attempts an interior realism of mental processes, not the conventional realism of external events. If we submit to the emotional flow of the film, accepting it as occurring in the present without worrying about understanding it intellectually, then it emerges as a very simple and direct film containing nothing gratuitous and with a clear structural pattern. *Marienbad* is a love story but one that is not concerned with the external behaviour of the lovers. Its subject is the ebb and flow of their emotions, the turmoil into which love throws them and the event which the narrator describes as being in the past (Last Year) and in another place (at Marienbad) is in fact taking place here and now.

L'Année Dernière à Marienbad is in essence a continuous flow of images, words and music, but like a piece of musical composition it has a distinct shape, which gives it its emotional impact, and can be readily broken down into five movements or stages. Firstly, there is the long and hypnotic opening tracking shot which seems to take us away from the real world into an enclosed universe, with its isolation emphasised by the baroque setting. The effect is reinforced both by the organ music composed by Francis Seyrig which accompanies this opening sequence and recurs constantly throughout the film, and by the voice of an initially unseen narrator, X, played by Giorgio Albertazzi: "Once again — I walk on, once again, down these corridors, through these halls, these galleries, in this structure — from another century, this enormous, luxurious, baroque — lugubrious hotel, where endless corridors succeed silent — deserted corridors overloaded with a dim, cold ornamentation of woodwork, stucco, mouldings, marbles, dark mirrors, dim paintings, columns, heavy hangings ... " This monologue too returns at several other points in the film, always slightly altered in content but the same in tone: measured, rhythmical, marked by a slight foreign accent and by theatrical diction and emphasis.

In the second section this voice mingles with the replies given in a play presented before the hotel guests and with the latter's conversation afterwards. It leads eventually to the words which may be said to conclude this part of the film: "You're still as beautiful ... But you hardly seem to remember." All the elements of the story to follow are contained in this opening. In the play fragment we find the basic situation of a man and a woman, both formally dressed, waiting until the clock chimes when the woman yields: "I am yours", and the play ends. It also contains the setting of much of the subsequent film: a balcony with a balustrade, a view over formal gardens and a statue. In the fragments of conversation among the guests which we overhear are references to extraordinary happenings, little mysteries and ambiguities, as well as a few concrete details such as a broken

96

L'ANNÉE DERNIÈRE À MARIENBAD: the three characters involved in the love triangle. Top, Sacha Pitoëff as M, the 'and', and below, Delphine Seyrig as , the woman, and Giorgio Albertazzi as X, the narrator.

L'ANNÉE DERNIÈRE À MARIENBAD: Giorgio Albertazzi, top, with Delphine Seyrig, and below, playing the game with counters against Sacha Pitoëff.

heel. Most important of all is the story of someone called Frank, told by one of the guests: "Don't you know the story? It was all anyone talked about last year. Frank had convinced her he was a friend of her father's and had come to keep an eye on her. It was a funny kind of eye of course. She realised it a little later: the night he tried to get into her room . . . " In this way the early part of *L'Année Dernière à Marienbad* represents a pre-creation chaos: all the elements are present, 'in the air' as it were, but they have not yet coalesced and focused on two individuals.

The film's third stage, that of the persuasion, begins with this, which comes with the first real conversation of the narrator, X, and the beautiful if statuesque woman A, played by Delphine Seyrig, who is now singled out from the anonymous mass of guests. X explains, in a tone reminiscent of an art film commentary (shades of *Van Gogh*!), the detail of a moulding and then refers explicitly to the theme of memory: "You hardly seem to remember me." The first 'memory' is then evoked: in the gardens of Frederiksbad (or perhaps Karlstadt, Marienbad or Baden-Salsa) there was a discussion on a balcony about a statue to be found there of "a man and a woman in classical dress whose frozen gestures seemed to represent some specific scene." This statue, coming after the play and the story of Frank, represents the film's third main focal point. First the details of the statue are evoked verbally by X, then in a subsequent meeting with A (who is discovered reading a book in a little salon) it is successfully 'visualised' and the gestures of A in relation to it 'directed' by X, as if A were an actress rehearsing a role. A later discussion of the statue centred on an engraving of the subject hanging on the hotel wall is dominated by M (A's mysterious guardian, played by Sacha Pitoëff) who authoritatively asserts that the statue is far from being mythological, allegorical or representing, as X has suggested, his relationship to A. Instead it depicts an historical subject, Charles III and his wife, the classical costumes being purely conventional. This intervention of M's is typical of his somewhat mysterious role in the film. His precise relationship with A is left in doubt and yet he seems to be always somewhere in the background. His repeated contact with X in the film takes the form of a succession of games in which he invariably wins. Nevertheless he finally emerges as loser in the struggle for A's mind. The exact significance of the game is difficult to assess if one follows the authors' injunction to avoid hunting for symbols, yet it clearly serves several purposes: its constant return is a further rhythmical element and it demonstrates the basic inadequacy of a logical approach (it is a game of skill not chance) in this dream-world of *Marienbad*.

The visualisation and acceptance of the statue represent X's first victory, the base on which he builds his persuasion, and it is significant that it is A who now prompts further revelations, saying, albeit in an ironic tone: "Tell me the rest of our story." The next two 'memories' evoked seem insignificant ones — a trivial conversation with friends somewhere and an incident of walking in the gardens with a broken heel — and A apparently accepts them in the course of the evening's dancing. But then X makes a further step forward: "At night most of all, you enjoyed not talking", and so provokes a sudden flash image, very bright, of a bare room. X continues inexorably: "One night I went up to your room", and A is shocked, horrified, and drops her glass. This is one of the film's moments of tension and a variant of it returns later at another instance of stress. The following part of the film, containing many confusing cuts and meetings shows the progress X makes in bringing A to remember (or to accept his version) through successive shots of the room which gradually changes from the empty whiteness of the initial flash to a more realistically furnished bedroom. This takes place in face of A's growing agitation, continued denial and reiterated desire to be left alone. X continues to impose his vision and the terms in which A rejects it: "I don't know that room, that ridiculous bed, that fireplace with its mirror", show that she has 'seen' it too. X interprets her fear in terms of M: "He's the one you're afraid of . . . Who is he? Your husband, perhaps," but it is really X himself and his story that terrify A: "No. Be still. Please. You're completely mad." Finally X achieves his end, A 'accepts' the garden, the walk with him, the broken heel and the return to the hotel.

With this something changes and the fourth stage, that of terror, begins. X's statement: "I've come now to take you away" still meets with a refusal but as he tells A it is now too late to refuse, and as if to prove his words we see the bedroom fully created, real, authentic, indubitably there. In this setting X tries vainly to persuade A to obey him as he tells her how she is to move. At this point X becomes for the first time a little uncertain, as if he too did not know the end of the story and he repeats three times: "No, I don't remember any more . . ." From now on any pretence at linear development is abandoned and a succession of mutually contradictory episodes occur one after the other. An attempt at proof with a photograph leads to the first possible *dénouement:* a scene of jealousy with M shooting A. X rejects this: "No, this isn't the right ending . . . I must have you alive," and A begs to be alone. There follows an alternative outcome, a rape, succeeded in the film as we see it (but not in Robbe-Grillet's script) by overexposed shots of A coming to meet X with arms outstretched over and over again. This too is rejected by X: "No, no, no. That's wrong." Another meeting in the garden takes place. This time it is dark and their clothing is over-elaborate (just as in an earlier 'unreal' scene the room has been over-furnished). Here another step forward is made, for A speaks the words he has claimed she spoke 'last year': "Next year, here, the same day, at the same hour . . . And I'll come with you, wherever you want." But the final outcome is again wrong: someone disturbs them and as X leaps over the balustrade it collapses, taking him with it. A's scream takes us back to the earlier scene by the bar when she dropped her glass. This time she goes off to bed alone and now the film is able to find its real resolution. After all the doubt and terror X is able to impose his ending and make A accept it. This 'true' ending begins as the film itself had begun with the narrator's voice: "And once again I was walking down these same corridors . . ." But now there is certainty: "I will leave tonight . . . taking you away with me." There comes the rather tender farewell scene of

100

M and A and then, while everyone else is at the performance of the play with which the film began, A obeys X's voice and prepares to leave. At midnight, but without saying a word to him, A leaves with X.

After the two of them pass through the door of the hotel we do not see them again but they have not escaped into the world of reality. The scene changes to the gardens with the hotel seen from outside at night. The voice of X is heard again making it clear that they are still trapped in a new labyrinth that has succeeded the hotel corridors: "The park of this hotel was a kind of garden *à la française* without any trees or flowers, without any foliage... Gravel, stone, marble, straight lines, marked out rigid spaces, surfaces without mystery. It seemed, at first glance, impossible to get lost here... at first glance... down straight paths, between the statues with frozen gestures and the granite slabs, where you were now already getting lost forever, in the calm night, alone with me." To the heroine one might apply another sentence from Borges ('The God's Script'): "You have not awakened to wakefulness, but to a previous dream. This dream is enclosed within another, and so on to infinity, which is the number of grains of sand. The path you must retrace is interminable and you will die before you ever really awake."

* * *

In *L'Année Dernière à Marienbad* any personal elements were subordinated to the conception of the film as an experiment in using the medium in new ways. It may be recalled that the first discussions of Resnais and Robbe-Grillet revolved around questions of form, not content. Furthermore, they both maintained a sense of distance from their work; as Resnais said, "Robbe-Grillet and I felt ourselves very much outside the film and we looked upon it as an object."[9] Given this sense of detachment it is hardly surprising that their conceptions should have diverged considerably, a fact that has given detractors of the film plenty of scope for adverse comment. What really needs to be examined though is the exact form these divergences take for this is the key to an assessment of the collaboration. If these two men, so different in temperament and background, were able to work without friction it is largely because their contributions were complementary. Of course Robbe-Grillet wrote the whole film, visualising the shots as well as composing the dialogue, and Resnais directed it all, shaping the playing and speaking as well as realising the images, yet their contributions can be separated.

Normally a film script is a pretty miserable thing, constantly forcing one to conjure up the images, but Robbe-Grillet's 'ciné-roman' has a quite unusual coherence. It is clear that approaching the film from literature, Robbe-Grillet has conceived his film in terms of a verbal persuading, that the narrator's words are half the film, its backbone as it were. Absorbing them we imagine the film from his point of view, while the images, being described but not actually seen, are much less forceful. From this angle such questions as: Did that man and that woman really meet and fall in love last year at

Marienbad? Does the young woman remember, and is she only pretending not to recognise the handsome stranger? Or has she really forgotten what there had been between them? are, as Robbe-Grillet tells us, quite meaningless.[80] All the emphasis falls on the act of imposing this version of events and the film has, in this light, quite a simple line of development, it all happens on one level, at one time and one place — as he talks — and to this extent the film is easier to read than to see.

The director, on the other hand, being primarily concerned with the images, was largely dealing with the woman's side of the affair, for the images belong to her principally, representing her thoughts and her relation to the man. From her point of view, and hence from the director's, there is no single certainty, rather the essence of the film lies in its ambiguity. Among the many explanations of the film put forward by Resnais[39], persuasion is only one of the possibilities. Others are that it is a film on the uncertainties of love or on parallel universes, about imagination or the difficulties of communication. Perhaps it takes place in an asylum or clinic and Resnais has said that M's words to A in their last scene together: "You should get some rest. Don't forget, that's why we're here," remind him of the end of *Caligari* when the doctor says: "Yes, he will calm down and I'll cure him."[9] Yet another possibility is the idea of an ancient Breton legend with Death coming to fetch his victim after a year and a day. In support of this one might quote the resemblances between the garden described in X's last words and a cemetery. But none of these explanations suffices and the film is of necessity open to divergent interpretations.

In so far as the film's images are a representation of the woman's stream of consciousness they contain varying shades of truth and *Marienbad* is indeed a "film about greater or lesser degrees of reality."[9] Since the woman finally comes to accept the man's account of the past as real, the *mise en scène* must be conceived in terms of a real past, for the images represent what is subjectively true, not what is objectively real. As Resnais put it: "I could not say to the actors: 'This scene that you are going to shoot means this. But it could equally well mean that, or even something completely different', I had to choose a solution, define, for example, the level of reality on which a scene took place." In the organisation of his shooting script Resnais had to 'untangle' the film and establish an external chronology: "For *Marienbad* we made a complete chronology on graph paper. And we always said, before beginning any scene with the actors: 'This scene follows such and such a scene on the level of montage, but it follows another scene which will appear much later in the film in terms of its degree of reality.' "[9] While this was a necessary procedure for the directing, it is in no way a key to the film's meaning, for this is inseparable from the actual order of scenes as they appear in the script or finished film.

In this way the approaches of Resnais and Robbe-Grillet diverged, indeed were bound to do so on account of their differing functions, but this divergence can only give the film an added power and impact, since its essence is the balance and opposition of image and text. The collaboration also allows two quite distinct cultural worlds to be brought together and startlingly fused. Robbe-Grillet's script, having close connections with the researches of the 'nouveau roman' and a concern with linguistic texture may be considered to have its roots in Kafka. It is matched by an equally rich visual texture, provided by Resnais, which is rooted in the cinema's past, the great experimental era of the silent film. Questioned by Pierre Billard about the resemblances between Delphine Seyrig and Louise Brooks or Garbo, Resnais made clear the extent to which his film drew on cinematic sources: "It is true that I wanted to recover a kind of fascination peculiar to the silent cinema. These 'quotations' which you mention were never intended deliberately in a specific shot. But we tried to obtain a silent cinema style of photography. We even went so far as to ask Kodak to manufacture again for us, a film that was not 'anti-halo', so that the whites would run. That did not prove possible, but by dint of evoking the silent cinema, we finished up impregnating the whole film with it."[39]

Robbe-Grillet's interview with 'Cahiers du Cinéma' began with the words: "An image is always in the present,"[40] and this defines one of the attractions of the cinema for him. Through his novels one can trace the gradual elimination of past and subjunctive tenses, so that his last two novels before *Marienbad*, 'La Jalousie' and 'Dans le Labyrinthe', are both written entirely in the present. They combine scenes that, logically, must have happened earlier or must be hypothetical, yet all are presented on the same level of reality by being described in the same tense. In literature this remains a somewhat artificial device, ignoring as it does a whole rich-ness of verbal expression, and it is perhaps for this reason

105

that Robbe-Grillet turned to the cinema, where the position is very different. On the screen there is only one tense, the present, for everything is presented as it happens. The reason why in the past flashbacks were always preceded by a dissolve and a title informing us that the hero or heroine is now remembering the past is that there is nothing in the quality of the following images themselves to indicate an earlier time. We have now become so accustomed to flashbacks that the dissolve is generally dispensed with, but no one before Resnais and Robbe-Grillet had made such a systematic use of this present tense quality of the film image. Whether or not Robbe-Grillet's psychological justification for the use of the present — that our imagination and memory function in this tense — is valid, this is certainly the way in which the cinema functions and a full realisation of this opens up new perspectives to the film art.

The effect on the concept of 'character' is startling. In conventional narrative characters are normally defined in terms of their past but here the possibilities of the past are explicitly denied. Delphine Seyrig, Giorgio Albertazzi and Sacha Pitoëff are therefore not playing characters who in the conventional sense have an existence before and after the film. Indeed it is truer to say that we witness the emergence of A and X out of the initial confusion and that by the end of the film they have disappeared again, for there is no sign of them in the final shot of the hotel exterior. Perhaps it is simplest to think of them not as people but as the complementary halves of a relationship, coming into existence when the relationship is born, being fused when it is resolved. Their total anonymity — they have no names, addresses, social ties etc. and the designations A, X and M are only adopted here, as in Robbe-Grillet's script, for convenience — is therefore their essence. In place of personal details and rounded characters comes a concentration on the play of emotion, in Resnais's words: "It is the feelings which interest us, the exchange of feelings between the characters, not the characters themselves. Perhaps there is only a single character. They have points in common and perhaps they are only one."[39] It is this flow of emotion that gives the film its impact and makes it a work addressed to one's sensibility rather than to one's intellect. The whole operatic style, diction and gesture, is conceived in this light and is a perfect solution to this acting problem for, just as in opera the gesture must be subordinate to the flow of the music, so here it must obey the flow of emotion.

Both Resnais and Robbe-Grillet have talked about the film in terms of realism and it is illuminating to examine the film's theme — the love relationship of the two main characters — in the light of this. Most of the so-called love stories of world literature, 'Romeo and Juliet' for instance, are much more concerned with the social consequences of falling in love than with love itself. It seems quite reasonable for a film intent on dealing with love alone to disregard matters of age, religion, morality, social status and so on, since a person in love tends to be indifferent to these anyhow. If one wishes to probe love, one must also get below the level of conscious life to the deeper impulses beneath, but for this there are no fully accepted literary or filmic conventions.

Those of the realism of social life — plot, character, setting — can be disregarded by the explorer of a realism of the mind for whom new forms are both inevitable and necessary.

The complexity of the film was a conscious step towards realism, as Robbe-Grillet's remarks show: "A passionate adventure, such as one sees in *Marienbad*, contains great areas of obscurity and ambiguity. I do not think that a work of art is made to remove these ambiguities or make these obscurities disappear. Why should a love story as it is related be clearer than a love story as it is lived?"[39]

The destruction of everyday logic and the creation of a new para-logic is achieved by the systematic and consistent reversal or extension of normal film techniques. To take a simple example, a flashback is conventionally used to take us into the past and then bring us back to our point of departure. In *Marienbad*, however, this clear cut division of past and present is blurred. For instance, there is a scene where X meets A reading in one of the salons. He talks about a meeting in the garden and we see A in a garden, wearing a different dress, but when we return to the salon we see A with her book again but retaining her outdoor clothes. A simple device like this makes the reconstruction of a 'real' chronology virtually impossible for the spectator but it does obey a logic of its own. A little anecdote by Resnais illustrates this perfectly. When he was talking one day to a girl who had just returned from India, he had a vision of her in a blue dress on the steps of the temple of Angkor. Any truly realistic depiction of their conversation which did not wish to keep merely to the surface would have to include this image.

Yet despite its subjective truth such an image might have no objective reality at all: in the case of Resnais, the blue dress was the one the girl was wearing when he met her and she had in fact never been to Angkor.

A similar freedom is shown in the handling of the interior monologue. We are accustomed in films to a split between image and text, to shots, say, of a girl walking along the street while a man's voice muses: Who was this girl I passed every day? Would I talk to her one day? What would her reactions be? Was she married? and so on. *L'Année Dernière à Marienbad* has a similar pattern of division but the roles of image and text have been reversed. Resnais chose a foreign actor speaking French with a slight accent to help the spectator realise that the inner monologue is not in the words, which here play a part analogous to the shots of the girl in the previous example. The stream of consciousness here is in the image "which even when it represents the past corresponds to the present in the character's head."[9] Here again, as so often in this film, the technique is the very opposite of literary since it aims at replacing with images what is, in the conventional cinema, verbalised and hence robbed of its true ambiguity. For Robbe-Grillet the latter is what must be captured at all costs: "The whole question is knowing whether the uncertainty attached to the images of the film is exaggerated in comparison with what surrounds us in our everyday life or whether it is rather of the same order. For my part, I have the impression that things really happen in this way."[40]

In June 1960, before work on *Marienbad* began in earnest, Resnais had told an interviewer that "the traditional recipes

109

of construction are only one of the possibilities of the cinema"[5], and in Robbe-Grillet he found an ideal collaborator quite happy to discard the whole framework of the linear plot. Whereas a conventional plot arranges the events in a 'vertical' pattern of logical sequence, Robbe-Grillet had come to favour a 'horizontal' pattern of variations on an initial situation. In the case of *Marienbad* it is clear that this latter is the system adopted: the elements of the plot are all revealed before A and X come together. The application of these story elements to the two characters is hindered by their reactions — A refuses her part, X at one time loses the thread of his argument, several possible endings are tried out before an acceptable one is found. Nor do the elements belong to A and X exclusively — they have found expression elsewhere, in the play fragment, the statue and the 'last year's' story of Frank which X seems to follow so closely.

The effect of the systematic use of variation and repetition is to produce a setting where nothing is stable or certain. On the one hand all the corridors, all the rooms, all the gardens, the past and the present, the real and the imaginary resemble each other. On the other hand, no one place is ever the same, the heroine's bedroom changing from bareness to normality and on to a rococo delirium. In a similar way seemingly significant incidents like the game played by M may be irrelevant, nothing but elaborate traps, while casual interrupted conversation, like that of the guests at the beginning, may contain the germ of the whole film. Robbe-Grillet had already insisted with regard to 'La Jalousie' that the meaning of the novel lay in the movement of the description, not in the thing described. Now in the cinema he could use the voice of a narrator to make this poetical movement of the language apparent and fuse its rhythms with those of Francis Seyrig's score and Resnais's images. Such a structure is clearly nearer to music than to the traditional forms of film and theatre, and in this sense is a development from and advance on *Hiroshima*, in that the musical pattern is now the only valid and meaningful one since all reference to external space and time have been destroyed.

To destroy spatial and temporal logic Resnais employs a number of logically 'impossible' tracking movements in which the same character occurs in two quite different positions. The use of an imaginary geography is quite common in the cinema and Resnais uses the same technique with the three baroque castles (Nymphenburg, Schleissheim and Amalienburg) that served as locations for *Marienbad*, but edits the fragments of the film in such a way that the same doorway constantly gives access to a new room and the garden is constantly changing, sometimes with paths and hedges, at others with pools and fountains, the same statue being found in a variety of places and occasionally absent from where it was before. In this way a labyrinth is constructed and indeed a whole spatial reality that has little connection with the world as we know it. At the end of the film too the characters cannot leave the suffocating atmosphere of the hotel for the real world, since they have no existence outside it. So the film ends with a new labyrinth and the 'disappearance' of the characters.

In like fashion, chronology is ruthlessly destroyed and Robbe-Grillet here carries out the programme announced in his essay 'New Novel, New Man': "Why should we try to reconstitute the time that belongs to clocks in a tale that is concerned with human time? Isn't it wiser to think of our own memory which is never chronological?"[50] Tampering with time is essential to the dramatic impact of a film and occasionally really imaginative use has been made of the cinema's potentialities, as when Max Ophuls in *Madame de . . .*, wishing to show a succession of different meetings, has a sequence of shots of a couple dancing, each successive shot being nearer than the last and depicting the pair in different clothes but all of them edited to form one dance and accompanied by a single waltz tune. It is precisely this kind of submission of events to a rhythm that Resnais employs in *Marienbad* but he no longer offers an external frame of reference. With the Ophuls film we can say: Oh yes, that depicts a succession of meetings spread over a week or a month. But with the Resnais film any such ambition is doomed to failure as the attempt of Jacques Brunius to cope with a similar scene shows: "One seems to be justified in assuming that this whole sequence is an evocation of the preceding year (Minus One) which would mean that the photograph was taken not last year (Minus One) but two years ago (Year Minus Two) or even before (Year Minus Three) and given to her last year (Minus One) in a previous attempt at persuasion" (in *Sight and Sound*, Summer 1962). Ultimately the only answer to the question. Where does the action take place? is 'on a screen' just as the only real duration of the

Top, the oppressive baroque setting.
Below, the opening play sequence.

Alain Resnais in thoughtful mood
during shooting of the film.

MURIEL: the tormented figure of Bernard (Jean-Baptiste Thierée) seen top with Françoise (Nita Klein).

events is the ninety minutes it takes for the reels to be shown.

This timelessness of the film as a whole throws into relief the one timeless element on which the story focuses, namely the statue (which was, incidentally, specially built for the film at the cost of a million francs and based on two characters in the background of a Poussin painting). Both the authors refer to it in explaining the significance of the film. Resnais said: "We wanted it to be as if we are in front of a sculpture which we look at first from one angle and then from another, which we now move away from, now draw near to."[9] Robbe-Grillet was more explicit and his words have a particular interest when one thinks of Resnais's shorts: "We can imagine *Marienbad* is a documentary on a statue, with interpretative views of the gestures, with a return each time to gestures themselves, such as they remain, frozen in the sculpture. Imagine a documentary that succeeded, with a statue of two people, in uniting a series of shots taken from different angles and with the help of different camera movements, and in telling a whole story in this way. And at the end you notice that you have come back to where you started from, the statue itself."[40] In this connection Jean Ricardou has given[105] a fine analysis of the double movement of the film, towards animation (the rococo decoration with its leaves and branches, the statue coming to life), and towards petrification (the stony garden at the end, the statue representing frozen movement). This is of course not a full explanation of the film but it is a sign of its visual and aural complexity. *Marienbad* represents the successful resolution of many of Resnais's stylistic preoccupations. It is "a film without psychologically defined characters in which the play of sentiments circulates just as in a contemporary painting the play of forms succeeds in being stronger than the anecdote."[9] Its total removal from everyday existence frees the acting from the needs of mere reproduction of gesture and allows, even demands, a complete stylisation: it is the acted film *par excellence*. Finally, its total disregard of "anecdote, witty dialogue, explanation or chronology"[3] throws into relief the rhythms of its images and soundtrack. In short *L'Année Dernière à Marienbad* is a film addressed simultaneously to eye and ear, satisfying to the emotions and stimulating to the intellect, a film in fact that "looks like a statue and sounds like an opera".[16]

6. Lazarus in our midst:
Muriel ou le Temps d'un Retour

> *But why can the Lazarian hero not enter a story? Everything becomes paralysed around his person. He keeps motionless, he is immediately panic-stricken when he is compelled to take part in any action whatsoever, to go on ahead, to experience a sudden change of fortune; he loses all his abilities. There is in a Lazarian narrative no story, no buoyancy, no plot. The characters go forward in leaps and bounds, sometimes cowering like beasts in the jungle, sometimes dying to be found, understood, loved. The hero of such a fiction is always on his feet, granted no respite, living only the outburst of a passion without following its progression or its rhythm, thoughtless, jostled, carried off into a multiplicity of episodes, a dispersal of the action, a sort of corruption of reality.*
>
> JEAN CAYROL: "Lazare parmi nous".

AFTER amplifying, in *Marienbad*, the dreamlike, non-realistic elements of *Hiroshima*, Resnais experienced the need for a complete change. While working on his second feature he had felt that much of its enclosed, suffocating atmosphere came from the impossibility of talking about Algeria, inherent in the subject as much as in the censorship situation of the French cinema. Furthermore, lacking Robbe-Grillet's absolute conviction of the futility of commitment in art, he not surprisingly wished for a return to everyday reality and to politics and action. The first of these needs was fulfilled in his work with Jean Cayrol on *Muriel*, which marks a radically new departure: an investigation into the possibilities offered by a realistic as opposed to oneiristic approach. Yet there is also a sense of continuity: as in *Hiroshima*, the past hangs heavily on the main characters, and as in *Marienbad* the real interest is in what happens inside the characters' heads. The novelty is that whereas in *Marienbad* the story was told from the inside, so that the spectator was given only mental images and left to invent the 'real' setting for himself, in *Muriel* the audience is given only the outside and made to deduce the emotions from purely external facts and gestures.

The scriptwriter of *Muriel*, Jean Cayrol, is an old friend of Resnais's and a man who, asked how long their friendship had existed, replied that he felt he had always known him.[56] The two had for years contemplated collaborating on a film. According to Cayrol[56], who in contrast to Resnais is a fervent Catholic, there was once a project to collaborate with Chris Marker on *La Vie du Christ*, but this advanced no further than an initial search for suitable locations. In the early fifties Resnais thought of filming his favourite among Cayrol's novels, 'La Noire', but at the time this too proved impossible. The idea was, however, taken up again later and then, as Cayrol has said, "something curious happened. One day Alain finally found the money to make 'La Noire', and he abandoned the project. He realised he could not enter an already finished creative work."[65] In 1955 came the collaboration on the documentary *Nuit et Brouillard*, much of the credit for which must go to Cayrol, and Resnais has recorded that, while making *Hiroshima mon Amour*, he often thought of the conversations they had had together on that film.[5] The first discussion of *Muriel* itself dates from 1959 although the film was in fact not shot until 1962-3. Jean

Cayrol's initial reputation had been established with several collections of poems and a series of novels which appeared after the war, for although he published some poetry earlier, his talent was crystallised by the Occupation years, when he fought in the Resistance, was captured by the Gestapo and spent four years in captivity, one at Fresnes and three in the Mauthausen concentration camp. His experiences there, reflected directly in *Nuit et Brouillard*, formed the background for his first postwar works in which he worked out his myth of Lazarus, the man who returned from the regions of death, which he set out explicitly in the two essays that together make up 'Lazare parmi nous' (1950). This same myth — generalised to a vision of contemporary life as a whole — underlies too, if indirectly, his work from 'La Noire' (1949) up to *Le Coup de Grâce* (1964). Interestingly enough Cayrol did once suggest of *Muriel* that "perhaps in this vision of things there is a relic of the concentration camp experience. Emerging from a drama, the detainee tries first of all to find his place in life once more. He is lost, like the man [in *Muriel*] who asks in a Boulogne street: 'Where is the centre?' and a woman replies: 'But that's just where you are'."[41]

Jean Cayrol had long been fascinated by the cinema, as he told an interviewer: "I'm passionately interested in the technical side. When I'm in the editing room it's a real drama, but I have a feeling of intense jubilation. And then I've always lived with the cinema: at the age of seven, I remember, I had the habit, at Bordeaux, of going along a little street because I would find bits of film in the gutters and dustbins."[56]

Like all Resnais's scriptwriters he takes the cinema very seriously — "For me writing and making films are two aspects of the same search"[56] — and in the sixties he has made, with Claude Durand, a number of short films, beginning with *On vous parle* (1960), and a feature film with marked similarities to *Muriel* called *Le Coup de Grâce* (1964). One of the themes which runs through all this work is that of memory and this, of course, brings him close to many of Resnais's central preoccupations. Of this aspect of his work Cayrol has said: "I write and make films to 'return': it's always the problem of memory regained. In 1943, in the train (going to the concentration camp) I lost my memory and struggled for hours. I suffer from an extraordinary amnesia: I have, so to speak, no childhood reminiscences, something which drives my mother to despair. I have worked a lot in time and on the theme of recollection."[56] This too, like his myth of Lazarus, finds clear expression in *Muriel*.

In his initial discussions with Cayrol, Resnais made it clear that he wanted in his film to do something he had not been able to do in *Marienbad*, namely have the characters concern themselves with the Algerian problem. He did not intend making an overtly political film, which in any case would have been impossible given the censorship situation in 1962, but he did want to deal with the surface of contemporary France. Cayrol began with the story of the older couple, Hélène and Alphonse, which, he tells us, is a true story which was unfolding at the very moment he spoke to Resnais about it but to which he has given an invented ending. Through the younger characters introduced to balance this pair he found

118

it easy to talk about Algeria. The collaboration of Cayrol and Resnais was close and intense and proceeded without any serious disagreement, for although Cayrol had ambitions to direct a film, he allowed Resnais a completely free hand: "He could do what he liked with my work: change it, move it around, destroy it. I deliberately gave him far too much. Sometimes five or six versions of the same scene, so that he could chose as he wished. He could have made several films with what I provided him."[65] During their months of work together Resnais gradually penetrated Cayrol's fictional world so that he could come to feel it. Later he tried to bring his actors to the same kind of understanding by having them read Cayrol's novels before the shooting began. Resnais's means of access were the characters, on whom Cayrol was made to expend great effort: "He was very much afraid that our heroes were only characters from a novel. He wanted to know everything about them, even things that don't appear in the film: have they a job? where do they come from? who were their ancestors? He made me justify every word and gesture."[65] Some of the biographical notes Cayrol prepared are to be found in the introduction to the published script and include details of, for instance, Hélène's parents and childhood and her wartime experiences. Resnais concerned himself with the overall structure of the film: "The idea of a script in five acts comes from him. It was a useful means of organising the work for, at a certain moment, we had to cut, articulate, put in order this mass of material. Knowing that the story would unfold in five acts it was easier for us to see the connections, the points of rising and falling tension.

119

Besides Resnais is very much influenced by the theatre. In the construction of a film what counts most of all for him is the dramatic element."[65]

Despite the fact that it is organised into five acts and that, in the published script, each shot is precisely situated in place and time, *Muriel ou le temps d'un retour* is very difficult to summarise adequately simply because it is so fragmented. In this respect it fully illustrates an idea of formal construction Resnais had discussed in 1961: "A classic film cannot translate the real rhythm of modern life. In the same day, you do twenty-six different things, you go to lectures, to the cinema, to your party meeting etc. Modern life is fragmented. Everybody feels that, painting, as well as literature, bears witness to it, so why should the cinema not do likewise, instead of keeping to the traditional linear construction?"[4] Certainly it is this fragmentation that strikes one most forcibly when one sees *Muriel* and few spectators would guess at first viewing that there is a division into acts. The whole action of the film covers a fortnight, from Saturday, September 29, to Sunday, October 14, 1962 and the form is completely symmetrical, with Acts One and Five each treating a single day, Act Three dealing with the central two days, while Acts Two and Four are each spread over a whole week.

The first act is focused on Hélène and begins with her going to the station to meet Alphonse, who was her first lover over twenty years ago when she was only sixteen and whom she has invited to Boulogne. She hardly recognises him and in any case he has arrived with a young actress, Françoise, ostensibly his niece but in fact his mistress. The three walk

120

back from the station, talking of nothing in particular, and in Hélène's flat make polite conversation over a meal prepared by Hélène (the first of several eating scenes in the film). When Hélène's stepson Bernard takes Françoise off for a walk down to the sea, Hélène and Alphonse make their first attempt to re-establish contact, speaking a little about the missing years, but Hélène, a compulsive gambler, rushes off to the casino with her current lover, De Smoke, and Alphonse is left alone to prowl around the flat and rummage through Bernard's belongings. The characters, split up in the course of the evening, drift back singly to the flat to sleep, except for Bernard who goes off to his attic workroom in the old part of the town. In the middle of the night Hélène and Alphonse continue their conversation and this part of the film ends on a note of peace, if not of concord.

Bernard is the centre of attention in Act Two. He has already, earlier in the film, made contradictory statements about his alleged fiancée Muriel and now we see several aspects of his life. These are mutually conflicting, for the tragedy of Bernard is that he cannot integrate the dislocated fragments of his existence. There is the Bernard who goes riding in the early morning along the cliffs on a white horse, a romantic-looking figure whom Cayrol's script compares to Ivanhoe. Then there is the happy, laughing Bernard with his 'good angel', his carefree young mistress Marie-Do. And, to set against these two, the Bernard who remembers Algeria and Muriel: "Nobody had known this woman before. I crossed the office where I was working, covered the typewriter. I crossed the yard. You could still see there.

121

"The shed was at the back, with the munitions. At first I didn't see her. As I went up to the table I stumbled over her. She seemed to be asleep, but she was trembling all over. They tell me her name's Muriel. I don't know why, but that couldn't be her real name. There were about five of us around her talking.

"She had to talk before night.

"Robert bent down and turned her over. Muriel groaned. She had put her arm over her eyes. They let go of her and she falls like a sack.

"It's then that it begins all over again. They drag her by the ankles to the middle of the shed to see her better. Robert kicks her. He picks up a torch and shines it on her. Her lips are swollen, full of foam. They tear off her clothes. They try to sit her on a chair, she falls off: one arm seems twisted.

"We had to make an end to it. Even if she'd wanted to talk, she would not have been able to. I joined in as well. Muriel whimpered as I slapped her. The palms of my hands burned. Muriel's hair was all wet.

"Robert lights a cigarette. He goes up to her. She screams. Then she fixed her eyes on me. Why me? . . . "

This is the memory that haunts Bernard and will eventually destroy him, and the recounting of it forms one of the film's most powerful moments. As we hear Bernard's words of horror and anguish, the images merely show his amateur films of army life in Algeria: scratched, ill-focused shots of soldiers and Arabs clowning and posing for the camera.

The middle part of the film, covering two days, shows the characters forced into action. Amid what is now the established routine of behaviour — Hélène bustling to and fro, Alphonse getting into conversations with everyone he meets in bars and restaurants, Bernard endlessly taking photographs — certain decisions are made. Hélène and Alphonse have to admit that their attempt has failed. Françoise decides to leave Alphonse when they return to Paris. At the restaurant meal on the Saturday, at which most of the characters are present, conversation is about change and uncertainty: Boulogne before and after the bombing, a prisoner returning after years of captivity, De Smoke's story of the house sliding imperceptibly down a hillside. The same evening two decisive encounters occur: Bernard comes face to face with Robert, his 'bad angel' who had pushed him into crime in Algeria, and Alphonse meets Ernest, who has frequently been seen in the background, apparently seeking someone, and who is now revealed as the brother of Alphonse's wife, Simone. The act ends on a note of fear with Hélène whispering into the telephone: "I'm afraid. What shall I do?" What the script calls the 'climate of panic' and 'atmosphere of malaise' increases in the fourth act, which covers the next week. The characters become lost in a multitude of trivial acts, other unknown characters seem momentarily significant and amid a succession of tiny, apparently meaningless scenes the tensions between Bernard and Robert, Françoise and Alphonse, Alphonse and Hélène, Bernard and Françoise grow more acute.

In the last act comes the explosion. Once more the setting is a meal, this time interrupted by Ernest. With his arrival the past bursts out to overwhelm the present. He sings, half

123

jestingly, half seriously, a song, 'Déjà', the lyrics of which refer explicitly to the situation of Hélène: "There is happiness to be had down here, but since people don't notice it, they prefer to fear the future, regret the past and say: already, already, already ..." Then he discloses the truth about Alphonse and his past, thereby provoking an ugly brawl. In the disorder, Bernard's tape-recorder is set working, he hears the burst of brutal laughter which brings back the Muriel experience in all its unbearable horror, and he rushes off to kill Robert. Françoise creeps quietly away. Ernest takes off Alphonse who eludes him, however, and boards a bus bound for Brussels. Hélène finds some sort of refuge with friends in the calmer, old part of Boulogne and so the characters are all dispersed, when Simone arrives. Her exploration of the empty apartment, followed by the camera in the only tracking shot of the film, brings *Muriel* to a close.

* * *

The basic theme of *Muriel* is the interaction of past and present — Hélène experiencing first love and Hélène at forty, Bernard as a soldier in Algeria and Bernard back home. Yet this theme is handled obliquely in the sense that there are no flashbacks in the film — every scene takes place between September 29 and October 14, 1962. The reason for this is that Cayrol, in all his fiction, is interested not so much in the dramatic moments of life — falling in love, becoming a torturer — as in the residue left by these experiences. As he himself has said: "Generally speaking, what interests me is not dramas. It is what happens afterwards. Not the going, but the coming back. How you return from a drama, how you pull yourself together. The characters of *Muriel* are people who do not 'pull themselves together'."[65] The full title of the film, *Muriel ou le temps d'un retour*, shows the importance given to this aspect of attempted reintegration into life on the part of characters who have survived a shattering experience. For the author, "the real suspense of *Muriel* is to know if they will be able to take root again, if they will be patient enough to be content with their memories, to adjust themselves to daily life, if they will be able to love quietly."[57] In very different ways Alphonse, Hélène and Bernard all have something they must come to terms with, and none of them succeeds completely. Bernard allows himself to be swamped by the past and driven to a murder that in no way alters the fact of his own complicity in torture. Alphonse prefers to avoid the complications of the past and instead to embroider his memories, using casual conversation with strangers to fill the void left by his refusal to face reality, and running off when things grow too complicated. Only Hélène, accepting the fact that her love for Alphonse was 'une histoire banale' and finding refuge away from the hubbub of her normal existence, has, at the end of the film, a chance of real reintegration.

The structure of *Muriel* was determined by the need to give adequate expression to these shattered and fragmentary existences. Despite the script's division into five distinct acts this is above all a jagged, abruptly edited film, full of jump cuts and startling transpositions, and thus ideally suited to evoke, for example, Hélène, of whom the script says at one point: "Hélène will not stop moving, coming and going. People will feel she is ill at ease, she is busy, loses herself in a thousand gestures, makes a mistake, comes back as if she had forgotten something." Just as the past is only indirectly evoked through the present, so the present itself is exposed only in tiny flashes: "*Muriel* is a film in facets, a film made up of mosaics . . . I think that Jean Cayrol and I adopted this form of narrative as soon as the script exceeded fifteen type-written pages. It is not something imposed at the editing, the shooting already corresponded to the final result."[23] Dis-cussing the evolution of the film Resnais found a striking analogy: "Gradually the characters began to come to life and it was then that we realised that we wanted to make a film of 'impregnation'. I rather like to compare it to a letter which is pressed on a piece of blotting paper. But we have only the illegible and obscure sentences on the blotter."[41] Certainly one of the characteristics of *Muriel* is that it gives us only part of any scene or sequence, character or truth, and we must learn to read between the lines if the film is to become com-prehensible. In contrast to *Marienbad* every action is rooted in everyday reality but the sense of strangeness is equally all pervading, simply because so much is omitted.

The whole narrative method illustrates this approach to reality. As Cayrol says towards the beginning of the script: "The story we are going to relate has no more importance than the other stories which may suddenly be born at a bend in the road or on a face. If this story takes on more importance than the others, it can equally well return to the anonymity of the crowd and city and disappear for a few moments." This is borne out throughout the film. We are given only fragments of the stories of Hélène and Bernard and even then Ernest comes to question much of what we thought we knew about Hélène and Alphonse. At one point Hélène feels that they have lost something by staging their reunion in the open, before the eyes of Bernard and Françoise: "It's a story that belongs to me, not to the others. And everyone comes and pokes his nose into it." Yet elsewhere she is only too aware of the similarities of her story and other people's — her response to Alphonse's account of his second love affair is: "But that's our story." During the fortnight or so that the film lasts, the characters live in close proximity — Françoise in Bernard's room, Alphonse in Hélène's sitting room — and three times they gather to have a meal together. Nobody in *Muriel* enjoys solitude or tranquillity. When the characters go out it is usually among people, in bars, cafés and restaurants. They are deeply influenced by the environment around them: Hélène summoned Alphonse because she heard someone talking in a voice just like his in the street, and Bernard has the shock of hearing an unknown woman call out: "Muriel, come here". It is never possible to be sure at first sight which characters are going to play a part in the story and which are mere 'extras' — all are presented initially in exactly the same way. Ernest emerges from the background to play a crucial role in the dramatic climax, but Robert's appearances in no way correspond to the importance he has in Bernard's life. Other characters merely put in brief appearances and hint at stories that might be told: the croupier at the casino, the man in search of the centre, the couple at the station.

Cayrol took great care with the choice of a setting for the film because the décor plays a vital role in bringing into relief the main themes: "I situated the story in Boulogne, despite Resnais's doubts, because Boulogne is also a town after a drama. There are two towns, the old one spared by the war and the reconstructed town, the topography of which the old inhabitants cannot recognise. I was very insistent on this theme. In Boulogne everything is false and at the same time everything is real. It's a town where you cannot settle for a moment. It's impossible to find your place there. This idea of searching for a place is very important for me. In the film, people and things move all the time. The furniture is always for sale. Hélène and Bernard cannot keep still for a minute. There is a perpetual malaise."[65] All the settings emphasise this, De Smoke's story of the house sliding down the hillside: "It's new, it's empty and people are waiting for it to drop. It won't make a good ruin", as much as Hélène's apartment where the dinner service used at the first meal has already been sold and the furniture constantly changing so that, as Bernard says, "You never know, when you wake up, if it's going to be Second Empire or Norman rustic style." Only the old part of Boulogne to which Hélène runs in her anguish seems to offer the possibility of stability but generally, as Cayrol says, the inhabitants "can live in their dramas, their adventures only as in costumes which are not made-to-measure but 'off the peg', dramas and adventures borrowed from other people."[91]

128

*MURIEL:
top, one of
the numerous
eating sequences
and, below, the
smiling, evasive
face of Alphonse
(n-Pierre Kerien).*

*MURIEL:
a growing
atmosphere
of terror
(Delphine Seyrig
and Jean-Pierre
Kerien).*

The camera style reflects the lack of harmony among the characters and between them and their environment. In place of the ample measured tracking shots of Resnais's later shorts and first two features comes a proliferation of tiny shots. Resnais told his cameraman, Philippe Brun, that the camera was to turn around the characters and objects like a fly and never come to rest,[73] and Cayrol too in the script specifies the style that Resnais and his crew have captured so well: "So we can have a camera fairly independent of the story, turning around the intrigues, fleeing, then returning like a restless animal." There are many examples in the film of startling effects achieved by this kind of staccato shooting and cutting, for example, in the first meal sequence when a cake is brought to the table and immediately — without transition — we see what is left of it when everyone has had a slice. Most striking of all are the shots used to illustrate the conversation about Boulogne as Hélène and Alphonse return from the station. Although the scene takes place at night, brief daylight shots are included which, according to Resnais, "seek to obtain a simple sensorial effect designed to alert the spectator's sensibility, put him in a state of uncertainty, even irritation, which fosters his lucidity of conscience."[41] Colour is also used for much the same reasons, "to help show up the mosaic aspect of the film by accentuating the breaks at each new shot."[41] It is part of Resnais's basic conception of the cinema that a film is ideally in colour, so that black-and-white is for him merely a further stage of stylisation not in any way indicative of a more direct and realistic approach. Resnais was greatly attracted by the idea of employing colour — usually kept for spectacular, historical subjects — in a film with a banal, everyday surface, and using it, moreover, without any concern to match shade and mood or achieve smooth harmonies and transitions within a sequence. He was, as he has said, concerned to "protest against the conventional notion of the greyness of everyday life, so that the colour was there to represent realism."[30]

Equally unconventional is the use made by Resnais and Cayrol of the soundtrack. Sounds themselves are used, as the editor Eric Pluet has pointed out, "to describe the town. Thanks to an abnormal soundtrack all Boulogne is present through sounds in Hélène's flat."[76] This playing of sound against image is typical of Resnais's method in *Muriel*. A similar example is the overlap of dialogue into the next scene, so that the voices we hear are frequently not those of the characters we can see at that moment. But most striking of all is the use of music as both a linking element and as a lyrical contrast to the banality of the images. Resnais had originally asked Cayrol "to write a few phrases evoking in a poetic manner the major themes of the film, notably those of memory, oblivion and recollection."[41] So the airs contain such ideas as 'Too much dead wood in our memory and the green wood extinguishes the fire', or 'time is torn like a letter one no longer dares to read again'. But set to music by Hans Werner Henze and sung by the soprano Rita Streich, they seemed to Resnais too explicit, and he preferred to have them recorded in such a way that the words are hardly distinguishable, a solution which he found to be ideal for a film where all the really important elements are evoked only indirectly.

As far as dialogue is concerned, Resnais had been troubled, while working on his unrealised project with Anne-Marie de Villaine, by the way in which everyday languages dates: "It's very difficult from the moment you accept making a fiction film with characters who express themselves through everyday language, it's difficult to make them speak properly in any everyday manner about immediate things, that is to say that the difficulty of this film called *A suivre, à n'en plus finir* is the following: the length of time between the moment of writing and the release of the completed film would have to be no more than a month, or a month and a half."[20] In Cayrol he found an ideal collaborator, fascinated by the rhythms of everyday speech, but with a poet's ear and ability to translate them into a work of art. Cayrol has said of his attitude to language: "I am personally very much aware of the way people talk. I listen a lot, in the street and in cafés. People say that everyday language is made up of commonplaces. That's completely false. On the contrary people's conversations contain an extraordinary poetry and invention. I wanted to try, as in my novels, to reproduce these remarks which are at one and the same time preposterous and banal. I've heard dialogues like those in *Muriel* twenty times. At the same time our characters had to speak a borrowed language, a language belonging to nobody just as their story is not theirs but belongs to everyone, is everyone's story."[65] A further element of complexity and counterpoint in the film is that this half poetic, half banal dialogue is presented in a manner that is deliberately made to clash with the content. The theatrical tone of the acting, particularly that of Delphine

Seyrig, and the use of stage gestures and mannerisms serve to emphasise once more the film's air of strangeness. It also follows *Hiroshima mon Amour* in preventing any sort of conventional identification with the characters: the lucidity of *Muriel* is in striking contrast to the hypnotic effect of *Marienbad* and in this respect anticipates the clear political commitment of *La Guerre est finie*.

On the surface a simple return to reality after the dream-world evasions of the earlier film, *Muriel* is in fact a work of great complexity, with its stylistic juxtapositions perfectly capturing the Cayrolian vision of reality. To convey its critique of conventional living and banal happiness — typified by the gastronomic preoccupations of the characters — *Muriel* uses a style in which the everyday is constantly undermined by the bizarre, platitudes given theatrical presentation, drab urban existence overlaid with lyricism and the humdrum photographed in glowing colour. In a world meaninglessly engaged on unceasing transition, where the old is uprooted and sold as a curiosity to tourists, the characters struggle vainly to come to terms with events that swamp them, to master passions that are out-of-key with their conventional responses. Yet the message of *Muriel* is not purely negative, for amid the chaos and ambiguity, the characters do preserve an essential freedom. In Cayrol's words, the authors "hope to show that everyone in *Muriel* is responsible for what he, himself, is — for what has happened to him. And that everyone must find his own way of life."[57]

132

7. Spanish Red: La Guerre est finie

> *Il chante pour tous les autres hommes le chant pur de la rébellion qui dit merci à l'amour, qui dit non à l'oppression.*
> PAUL ELUARD: "Guernica."

> *He called me a Spanish Red, and now, suddenly, I'm no longer alone in this grey innocuous room. From one end of the waiting room to the other I saw the expressions open and flower, saw the birth, in all that grey, of the most beautiful smiles in the world.*
> JORGE SEMPRUN: "Le Grand Voyage".

IT WAS in 1964, when he was already working actively on two projects of a very different sort, *Les Aventures d'Harry Dickson* and *Je t'aime, je t'aime*, that Resnais telephoned Jorge Semprun to suggest collaboration on a film. He had already read Semprun's novel, 'Le Grand Voyage', in which he had found much that indicated a certain unity of interests. The book's hero is a Spaniard leaving his homeland after the Civil War (cf. *Guernica)*, deported to Auschwitz by the Nazis (cf. *Nuit et Brouillard)* and a convinced Marxist (cf. the left wing politics of, say, the Japanese in *Hiroshima*). Above all Semprun's novel is a study of memory, for, in recounting his six-day journey to the concentration camp, the hero relives his whole life in non-chronological sequence. Two quotations will give the flavour of this aspect of the book. Firstly, the narrator talking about his arrival at Auschwitz: "Still today, in unexpected ways and at most extraordinary moments, that spectacle explodes in my mind. You're tossing the salad, voices are reverberating in the courtyard, some tune too perhaps, unbelievably coarse;

133

mechanically you toss the salad, you let your mind wander in the heavy, insipid atmosphere of declining day, of courtyard noises, of all those interminable minutes which are a whole other life, and suddenly, like a scalpel slicing cleanly into the soft tender flesh, this memory explodes, greatly exaggerated, terribly out of proportion." Or again, in contrast, the struggle to recall: "For sixteen years I've been trying to seize those few hours between the conversation with the guy from the Taboo underground and the maniacal night awaiting us, trying to pierce the haze of these few hours which obviously must have passed, to seize piece by piece the reality of these hours, but almost in vain. Sometimes in a flash I remember not what happened, for nothing ever did, at any time during this voyage, but the memories and dreams that plagued me or filled my mind during these missing hours, that are missing in the perfectly remembered recollection of this voyage . . . "

In his original conversation with Semprun, Resnais put forward two possible themes, a Greek political prisoner working on behalf of his comrades not yet released or the efforts of a committee for peace in Vietnam or Algeria. It was Semprun who, realising that the director wanted a specifically political film, insisted on Spain. Initially it proved difficult to organise the film, but a text by Sartre (used as epigraph in the published script) acted as catalyst: "The militant does not ask his act to justify him: he does not exist first to be justified later. But his personality encloses its own justification since it is constituted by the end to attain. So he is relative to the action which in turn is relative to the goal. As for the action itself it must be called an undertaking, for it is a slow

134

tenacious work of enlightenment which lasts indefinitely." Even then many months of work and three separate versions totalling about a thousand pages were needed before the script was finally completed. It is notable that though the film was based firmly on political reality, Resnais sought a certain idealisation of the characters' relationships as the scripting progressed. As Semprun has said: "Alain was very insistent that the film's meaning should not be exclusively negative. The film became more serene, calmer, more relaxed. I'm thinking, for example, of the relationships between Diego and his wife, and between Diego and reality."[66] Otherwise the collaboration followed the established pattern, with Resnais writing nothing but influencing the film profoundly.

* * *

La Guerre est finie follows what is now the familiar course of an action falling into five fairly distinct sequences, with, in this case, the first and last forming a framework for the crucial central scenes.

The film begins, as it will end, with the crossing of a frontier. Diego (Yves Montand) is returning to Paris to warn his comrades that the Spanish police have uncovered their organisation in Madrid and the identity of one of their leaders, presumably Juan. There is an unexpected police check at the frontier but Diego, relieved at getting through, pays little heed to it. To his driver Jude and Jude's wife he explains how the René Sallanches identity he uses is completely authentic except that his, Diego's, photograph is substituted in the passport.

135

As he heads back to Paris, he is thinking of Juan and of Nadine Sallanches, whom he has never met but whose quick wits on the telephone have just saved him. These opening scenes, and some later ones, are accompanied by the voice of a narrator (Jorge Semprun himself) who addresses the hero like his double, at once involved in and standing back from the action.

The following day begins with Diego in the suburbs — Ivry, Aubervilliers, Issy-les-Moulineaux — searching vainly for Juan, telling Carmen her husband has been caught in Madrid and contacting his old friend Ramon and his superior Roberto. But most of this Sunday, which makes up the second section of the film, is devoted to Diego's personal relationships, firstly with Nadine (Geneviève Bujold) whom he visits and makes love to, then with Marianne (Ingrid Thulin), his mistress for nine years and virtually his wife. With her he finds love of a very different kind, for she is someone with whom he can, for once, be honest and to whom he can pour out all the doubts and uncertainties that fill the tangled web of truth and deceit which is his life. Diego's report to his superiors about Madrid forms the core of the third part of *La Guerre est finie*. His ideas are coolly received and rejected as the subjective vision of someone too close to see the situation in perspective, while his departure from Spain is condemned as a decision taken too lightly. His thesis, that the impetus for change must come from within Spain and that a general strike organised from outside will be a failure, wins no support among his fellow exiles and he is told to rest and learn self-criticism. Returning the

Sallanches passport to Nadine he realises that the police are watching her but his efforts to help merely result in his being left with a suitcase full of plastic bombs to take care of. By evening his nerves are frayed, he sees his life's work as futile and he contemplates giving up everything and returning to Spain as a private citizen.

But next morning Diego is once more swept up in the action, finding himself compelled to defend his views to Nadine's young friends, who favour indiscriminate violence, and being sent after all to Spain, in place of Ramon who has died of heart failure in the night. Ramon's death makes him overcome his sense of defeatism — he imagines his funeral as a triumph of solidarity and resolves to look at Spain as if through the eyes of Ramon who would have been making his first return to his native land. Diego is again caught by a sense of belonging, of forming part of a human chain. As the narrator says: "One last time you will knock on doors, strangers will open them, you will say something or other, that the sun rises over Benidorm or that the almond trees are in bloom in the garden of Antonio, and they will let you in, and you will be together, for these are the pass words." But in fact Diego is heading for disaster. A police visit to the Sallanches's home makes it clear to Nadine that Diego, not Juan, is the man the Spanish police are following and the film ends with Marianne flying off to Barcelona to warn him of the danger.

*   *   *

137

La Guerre est finie is the first of Resnais's films to be primarily about a man, and this change of focus brings with it a wider scope. Instead of being solely concerned with the emotional life of his characters, Resnais is here concerned with the relationship between love and masculine (and, more specifically, political) activity. There is a noticeable change of tone also: his earlier heroines had been played by Emmanuelle Riva and Delphine Seyrig, actresses trained in the theatre to compose a role, but here Diego Mora is portrayed by Yves Montand, to whom the customary filmic understatement and 'realistic' performance are second nature. The portrait that forms the central part of *La Guerre est finie* is complex, but only because of the large number of facets, the full range of attitudes and contradictions included, not because of any tension between dream and reality (as in *Marienbad* or *Hiroshima*) or between the character and the mode of portrayal (as in *Muriel*).

First of all, Diego is a Spaniard. What this means to him is made clearest in his outburst to Janine and Bill, the friends he finds with Marianne when he arrives at her apartment: "Wretched Spain, heroic Spain, romantic Spain: I can't stand it any longer. Spain has become the lyrical good conscience of the whole left: a myth for old soldiers. Meanwhile fourteen million tourists are going to spend their holidays in Spain. Spain is no more than a tourist's dream or the legend of the civil war. All that mixed with the plays of Lorca, and I've had enough of the plays of Lorca: sterile women and rural dramas, that's quite enough. And the legend too, that's quite enough! I wasn't at Verdun, I wasn't and I wasn't at

Teruel either, nor on the Ebro front. And those who are doing things in Spain were not there either. They are twenty and it's not our past that makes them act but their future. Spain isn't the dream of '36 any longer, but the reality of '65 even if that seems disconcerting. Thirty years have passed and the old soldiers get on my nerves." It is to Spain that he dreams of returning when it seems for a while that his political activity has come to a halt, yet his relationship with his native land is at best ambivalent. Long years of exile have cut him off from his roots and to the driver who comments on his perfect French, he admits that sometimes he forgets that he is Spanish.

The rootlessness of Diego is emphasised by the fact that Spain itself is never shown in the film. All the action takes place in France at Easter 1965 and we see not the six months of Diego's active life in Madrid, but his three days of uncertainty in Paris. Nevertheless a thesis about the future of Spain is propounded in *La Guerre est finie*, the thesis of Diego the revolutionary who has spent twenty years of his life working for the overthrow of Franco. The significance of the film's title is that while one form of fighting is finished, the struggle must continue, and the film is specifically concerned with how exactly this may best be done. The variety of approaches is meant by Resnais to show "the lack of co-ordination and contact that exists in the anti-Fascist organisation" which "inevitably leads to misunderstanding and inefficiency."[37] There are, on the one hand, Diego's contemporaries, balding, middle-aged men who have spent half their lives in the suburbs of foreign cities, and who cling with misguided optimism to methods proved futile by a quarter of a century of failure. Diego criticises their idea of a general strike and to Marianne he describes their leaflet addressed to the Spanish workers as "a kind of magic language, as if they took idols in procession to make the rain fall." Diego's views are formulated by the narrator: "You also deny that the date and conditions of an action which is to take place in Spain can be decided in exile. We cannot put ourselves in the place of the workers of Bilbao, Barcelona and Madrid, make decisions for them." To contrast with this traditional view is that of Nadine's young friends, the self-styled Leninist group of Revolutionary Action, who like Diego reject the notion of a general strike, but favour indiscriminate violence aimed at destroying Spain's reputation as a 'normal country' and tourist paradise. Both groups, old and young, quote Lenin but, as Diego affirms, "Lenin is not a prayer wheel" and neither offers a satisfactory answer, at least in the eyes of Diego and the authors.

La Guerre est finie aims to provoke the spectator, make him question his comfortable assumptions about Spain and the left, and in this it shares the same tone as Resnais's other films. But it also puts forward an assertion — that it is in Spain that things will happen — and this is unusual, for Resnais had previously been content to state the question and had not tried to offer solutions. He and Semprun do provide a considerable degree of support for their view: they built their film around reality — the strike called for April 30 is a real one, as is the leaflet Diego reads to Marianne at the height of his disillusionment — and they assumed, rightly, that the exiles' plans would meet with failure. But their view remains a thesis one is free not to accept and which taken to its full consequences renders Diego's activities increasingly futile. His chief's criticism of Diego, namely that his reasoning is purely negative, contains a large degree of truth and the film provides no answer to his problem of how he, as an exile, can make a valid contribution to the cause of freedom in Spain. It is perhaps for this reason that the key political discussion between Diego and his colleagues — unlike his confrontation with Nadine's friends — has a muffled impact.

A further contributory factor to the somewhat negative effect of the film is that Diego, as well as being a Spanish exile and a revolutionary, has also reached the age of forty, a time of personal crisis when action for its own sake no longer proves automatically satisfying and certain questions seem unanswerable. He finds himself doubting the methods of his organisation, being tempted by the idea of opting out of the struggle, and lured into adventures that threaten his position. If, as he says, patience and irony are a Bolshevik's principal virtues, his own patience is wearing thin: "That makes twenty-five years that every minute has counted." Not only are the decisions becoming more difficult and the problems left unresolved — such as that of his relationship with Marianne — becoming more acute, he is also losing his grip. As Marianne aptly says: "You seem to be groping your way, Diego, to be in a fog, not knowing any more where you are going." Despite his imperturbability at the frontier and his quick sensing of a trap when he visits Nadine for the second time, he finds himself making mistakes that could easily cost him his liberty. He fails to switch on the lights when driving with a case of plastic bombs in the car, and gets stopped by the police. Above all he fails to realise that the man the Spanish police are trailing is not Juan but himself. Wrapped in his sense of invulnerability after twenty years of clandestine activity, he fails to pick up the tiny clue at the frontier (that the police know he has come from Madrid) or even to report this to the organisation. The references in *La Guerre est finie* to Jacques Becker — the photographer Bill's close resemblance to the director and Nadine's address in the Rue de L'Estrapade — are a reminder that one of the French cinema's finest portrayals of the ageing man of action was *Touchez pas au grisbi*, in which Jean Gabin played a gangster trying to make a last coup that will allow him to retire comfortably.

Something else which Diego shares with Becker's convicts and gangsters is the importance in his life of male friendship. Comradeship is the most important thing his life of political activity gives him. When Marianne questions him about giving up his present way of life he replies: "I should miss Spain, really. Like something you really miss, the absence of which is going to become unbearable... The comrades... The strangers who open their doors to you and who recognise you and whom you recognise. You are together." Through the film stretches a chain of men linked together by a common aim that Diego shares: Sallanches who lends his passport, Jude who acts as chauffeur, Antoine the contact at Hendaye station, Roberto, the Chief, Ramon, the anonymous comrade making false passports, Manolo, Sarlat who drives Diego back to Spain. It is with the aid of this human chain that Diego hopes to save Juan and is himself saved, a chain which, in moments of crisis, the women join too: Carmen, the wife of the imprisoned Andrès, Nadine and finally Marianne herself. For Diego, the exile, a sense of belonging is very important, and is provided by what Semprun called "this kind of network of solidarity, this very modest, very everyday aspect of what is called in books internationalism, but which is very real."[56] This comradeship is what carries Diego through his crises, makes him continue even when the struggle seems futile. His comrades in prison must know that the fight for freedom continues and, as he returns to Spain, the narrator aptly says: "You know very well that there will be no strike in Madrid on April 30. But you are caught up again by the fraternity of long and doubtful battles, by the obstinate joy of action."

One thing which his political activity cannot give him, however, is a real identity. Before he reaches Marianne's apartment we have already seen him in several guises: as an anonymous passenger to Jude, as René Sallanches to the police, as Carlos to his comrade Antoine and as Domingo to Nadine. To the latter he admits: "Sometimes I jump when someone calls me by my real name", and then proceeds, almost automatically, to give a false name — the day of the week in Spanish — as they talk after making love. It is not until the scene of his meeting with Marianne, when she repeats his name, that he is seen in his true identity, with someone who knows who he really is. Yet even Marianne had had to go through numerous aliases — Francisco, Rafael, Carlos — before getting to know him, and when she flies off to Barcelona to rescue him he is masquerading under yet a new name, the ludicrously inappropriate one of Chauvin. Changing his identity this frequently, he is adept at lying and does so even over tiny things, even to Marianne. To the driver who takes him back to Spain he suggests they pass the time telling their life stories, adding: "The false one as far as I'm concerned. The real one is unimportant." So it is hardly surprising that his life becomes so difficult for him when he begins to question its meaning and purpose.

To complicate matters still further Diego's life with Marianne is not a secure identity offering real integration with society. For one thing it clashes with his political activities. "Falling in love is not foreseen in the life of a professional revolutionary," he tells Marianne, who is only too aware of the hostility her elegance arouses in Diego's comrades. His affair with Nadine is perhaps a symptom of his lack of satisfaction with life. He deceives Marianne by keeping silent about this, even though Nadine was "only a momentary desire and pleasure. Not happiness unsatisfied because of its inexhaustible richness, but a fleeting satisfaction, perhaps and above all the satisfaction of his masculine pride." Moreover, though his love for Marianne has lasted nine years, they have not married and still, to her sorrow, have no children. Her earlier marriage, though ending, one assumes, disastrously, did leave her with a son to love and care for, but if Diego were arrested she would be left with nothing but her memories. With him she has no real social life, home or

Hélène (Delphine Seyrig), seen here with De Smoke (Claude Sainval), finds refuge in the old part of the town at the end of MURIEL.

LA GUERRE EST FINIE: the richness of Diego's relationship with Marianne (Yves Montand and Ingrid Thulin).

LA GUERRE EST FINIE: Diego's encounter with Nadine (Yves Montand and Geneviève Bujold).

family existence, a state emphasised by the fact that they are both exiles, she Swedish, he Spanish, rootless individuals who met in Rome and now live, when together, in Paris. The need to lie to friends like Janine and Bill, the nagging little remarks of Agnès ("I wondered if you really existed . . . ") lead Marianne to despair at times: "It's our life that seems like a lie. Didn't you hear Agnès? A false couple with a false life." There is poignancy in the fact that she is editing a book on "the way the city speaks to its inhabitants and how the people in the street reply to it", because she will never have this sense of unity with her environment. The two disparate halves of Diego's life, the personal and the political, are united at the very end of the film when it is Marianne who is sent to Spain with the password 'The sun is rising over Benidorm', but such a fusion can be no more than temporary and in the film, as in life, the real problems remain unsolved.

Diego Mora, then, dominates the film with his thoughts, actions, memories and anticipations. Only once in *La Guerre est finie*, the single tracking shot following Marianne into the kitchen while he sleeps on, do we get a scene from which he is absent, elsewhere it is his "eyes, gestures and acts which give the world a structure, a psychological reality." Faced simultaneously with the problems of love and politics, Diego emerges as a complex character, ambiguous in the way that Resnais likes his heroes and heroines to be. This splendidly realised central character, excellently portrayed by Yves Montand, gives *La Guerre est finie* a fine coherence and has prompted Resnais to some fruitful stylistic experiment. The use of anticipatory flashes, totally realistic because that is the way Diego sees life, is original and succeeds in giving the opening of the film a disorientating, thought-provoking atmosphere reminiscent of *Muriel*. Resnais has differentiated well the two kinds of love experienced by Diego in scenes that were not described in the script but improvised with the actors. On the one hand the essentially loveless, cerebral affair with Nadine is conveyed by almost abstract shots — strongly reminiscent of Godard's *Une Femme Mariée* — of isolated thighs, hands, bodies shot against a neutral background and given an ethereal musical accompaniment. On the other, the warmth and passion of Diego's love-making with Marianne is conveyed by shots of real sensuous bodies seeking each other and the scene is reinforced by being accompanied by the principal lyrical theme, which is also used for Ramon's funeral. As always in Resnais's films, the performances he extracts from his actresses are quite superb. A fine unity is also given to the film, despite its wealth of divergent material, by its rigorous organisation into five acts, three days and a framework pattern provided by the two frontier crossings.

What *La Guerre est finie* lacks is a certainty of tone. It is not by chance that this is Resnais's only feature film where filmic references are obvious, even obtrusive, or that the script needed to be entirely rewritten twice and was still changed quite extensively during shooting. Semprun, the author of only a single novel, does not possess the markedly personal literary style and 'universe' that all the previous scriptwriters have had. The subject and script with which he furnished Resnais demanded a purely realistic treatment: all scenes are timed, located and dated exactly; the authors have tried to situate the film as near as possible to the time of writing so as to achieve complete contemporaneity; Yves Montand who dominates the film gives a naturalistic, not theatrically stylised performance; the camera style with its seven hundred and fifty different set-ups, is bare and functional; even the imagined scenes are quite realistically presented. Yet this kind of approach is not Resnais's forte, and the film does not develop in any new way the stylistic concern with an interplay of text, image and music which has been the director's greatest contribution to contemporary cinema. The musical score, though by Giovanni Fusco, is the least inspired of any of Resnais's films and one misses the poetry with which Jean Cayrol could infuse the realistic subject matter of *Muriel*. *La Guerre est finie*, a prosaic film *par excellence*, furnishes the counterbalance to the pure cinematic poetry of *L'Année Dernière à Marienbad* and though it undoubtedly reflects one side of its author's complex personality it is not altogether surprising that it left him dreaming of "a film where a language like that of Shakespeare or Giraudoux will be heard."[35]

147

8. Themes and Variations

Le cinéma, c'est l'art de jouer avec le temps.

ALAIN RESNAIS

SINCE Alain Resnais is still only forty-five and has completed so few feature films, it is premature to attempt a summing up of his achievements or an evaluation of his impact on his contemporaries, though both are clearly considerable. But having examined his idea of the director's role and his conception of the cinema as the interplay of aural and visual rhythms, and having followed his progress chronologically to see how his childhood preoccupations shaped his later film-making, just as his documentaries served as testing grounds for ideas to be fully developed in his features, we are left with one task: that of assessing his role as non-writing but omnipresent partner in the composition of his film-scripts. A recent scriptwriter, Jorge Semprun, remarked somewhat wryly of his work on *La Guerre est finie:* "Through all the detours of a seemingly groping advance, through the successive versions of a script — which are superimposed like geological strata — the original intentions of Resnais become explicit and you find yourself busy writing more or less well, just what he has intended you will write."[66] If this is true — and other collaborators have expressed much the same sentiments, Ghislain Cloquet saying, for instance: "All those who have worked with Resnais have the feeling of having been dominated, but dominated in an agreeable fashion: broadened, multiplied"[72] — then it is fair to seek, in the four feature films we have hitherto considered

separately, a coherence that extends beyond the purely stylistic unity which they so evidently possess and which has,
I hope, become apparent in the course of this study. Each of
the four is a remarkably original work — one can never
anticipate what Resnais's next film will be from one's knowledge of the previous ones — and all clearly exhibit the tone
and style of their accredited authors. Moreover, it is this
aspect of them that Resnais, always anxious to deny or conceal the personal element in his work, has invariably stressed.
Yet when one looks more deeply, the thematic homogeneity
they display is remarkable.

In essence, and despite their surface disparity, Resnais's
films return again and again to the same basic inter-related
themes which are, characteristically, those underlying much
of the more significant art of our century. Firstly, there is the
obsession with time, amply witnessed by the fact that each
of the feature films is in a single tense in the grammatical
sense: *Hiroshima* in the past, *Marienbad* the conditional,
Muriel in the present and *La Guerre est finie* the future. In
spite of Resnais's denial of any conscious intent, his films
return time and again to the theme of memory and forgetfulness: on a collective level in the documentaries, with their
emphasis on the key disasters of our century that must not
be forgotten, and on a personal one in the features, which so
often show characters trying to come to terms with their own
past. Subjects like *Guernica* or *Nuit et Brouillard* could hardly
be treated other than as tracts on 'the evident necessity of
memory', but even material which at first sight appears intractable — the manufacture of plastics or the working of a

149

library — has the habit of taking shape as an essay on time or memory. Virtually all the feature film heroes and heroines are in their thirties or forties, old enough to have a stock of memories which can return to haunt them (the actress, Hélène, Bernard) or continue to shape their lives (Diego), and even in *Marienbad*, where chronology is destroyed, the narrative takes the form of the imposition of a memory, a past, on an unwilling woman.

This double dimension, past and present, gives richness to the emotional life of the characters which is so important to Resnais who has, in effect, furnished us with four studies of the possibilities of love. The ebb and flow of the characters' emotional responses, as they are torn between past and present, memory and oblivion, doubt and certainty, find apt expression through the essentially musical patterns of film structure which he adopts. There is no real concern with the moral issues involved — the authors of *Marienbad* never bother to specify whether M is husband or lover, guardian or brother, and Diego is in no way censured for his behaviour with Nadine — nor is there any integration of lovers and society. In Resnais's work love does not lead to the conventional 'happy' ending of marriage, children and family life, it remains a passion that momentarily engulfs the characters but leaves them with no more than their memories afterwards. In retrospect it may, for a time, appear 'an inconsolable memory, a memory of shadows and stone' or suddenly be rendered trite (to Hélène) or novelettish (to the actress) by being viewed in a social context. Love does not unlock the hotel prison of *Marienbad* nor satisfy Diego's cravings for

150

action and adventure, but it remains a driving force for the characters in all of Resnais's films.

The lack of interplay between the lovers and their environment is emphasised by their essential anonymity. In the situations in which we meet them they have no roots — they are abroad *(Hiroshima)* or in exile *(La Guerre est finie)*, resident in a hotel *(Marienbad)* or living in a town whose fluctuating décor denies their need for security *(Muriel)*. Often even that fundamental of human identity, the name itself, is missing: the lovers of *Hiroshima* and *Marienbad* are nameless, while Diego and Alphonse have only too many false lives and aliases. If the use of the words 'Hiroshima' and 'Nevers' serves to give an added, though supra-personal, dimension to the lovers in Resnais's first film, the adoption of the false names of Domingo and Nana brings out the lack of real contact between Diego and Nadine in *La Guerre est finie*.

The world around them offers no haven to these restless individuals, for it is an enclosed, suffocating universe in which they live (Robbe-Grillet, Cayrol and Semprun all use the phrase *monde clos* in their scripts to describe the characters' environment). Cayrol, the only writer Resnais has worked with twice since his art film days, is one whose vision takes contemporary society to be an extension of the concentration camp universe, and the prison image has continually haunted the director from the asylum of St. Rémy to the camp of Auschwitz, from the Bibliothèque Nationale, in which books are entombed, to the cellar at Nevers and the hotel at Marienbad. The lovers in the latter film escape only into a fresh labyrinth and even those who can walk in the streets are not free:

151

hanging over them is a shadow, that of Burgos jail for Diego, that of the past for the actress, Hélène and Bernard who cannot be rid of what happened last year, or fourteen, twenty, thirty years ago.

This sense of imprisonment is enhanced by the fact that Resnais's films are not directed outwards to the world around him but, since *Van Gogh* in 1948, have been used in "an attempt, still very crude and primitive, to approach the complexity of thought, its mechanism."[40] This inward movement is even reflected in his camerawork, for his characteristic camera movement is not the 'pan' from a fixed point but the tracking shot advancing into a painting, a building, an imaginary world. Resnais has often said that he aims at a realism that includes thoughts and mental images as well as conversation and surface behaviour, and the structure of all his films reflects this. In *Hiroshima* the action takes place in the woman's mind, the images of Nevers are *her* memories, surging up in *her* mind, while in *Marienbad* we have a virtual stream of consciousness so that everything seen, whether true or false, is shown as it passes through someone's mind. *La Guerre est finie* gives us mental images — Diego's thoughts about the unknown Nadine, his anticipations of Ramon's funeral, his fears about Juan — and only *Muriel* keeps rigidly to the surface, though even here, to appreciate the film, we must read the signs that show us what is going on inside Hélène and Bernard.

The continued vitality of Resnais's work is amply borne out by the two very different films on which he has worked since the bulk of this study was written. The first of these, **Loin du**

Vietnam (1967), a return to the documentary genre after an absence of some nine years, constitutes both an eloquent reminder of his conception of the cinema as an art based on collaboration and the culmination of the interest in politics already evident in *Muriel* and *La Guerre est finie*. *Loin du Vietnam* grew out of the scheme whereby Frenchmen were asked to contribute one day's pay to help the victims of the Vietnam war. Those, like Chris Marker, who found this insufficient, evolved the idea of making a film of protest against the war and presenting it to the Americans in the hope of influencing those actually responsible for dropping the bombs. The film involved six directors — Jean-Luc Godard, Joris Ivens, Claude Lelouch, Agnès Varda and William Klein as well as Resnais — in addition to dozens of reporters and technicians. Originally it was intended to be a purely collective effort in which individual contributions would remain anonymous and be inextricably interwoven by the editing (the credits do not differentiate between the functions of the various collaborators), but not surprisingly in view of the marked personalities of the directors involved, the film falls into a number of distinct episodes, despite the unifying effect of Chris Marker's commentary.

Resnais's own section, written with Jacques Sternberg, can easily be distinguished since it forms such a marked contrast to the rest of the film. It features the actor Bernard Fresson (who played the German in *Hiroshima mon Amour*) as a left-wing intellectual faced with the task of reviewing Herman Kahn's book "On Escalation". Watched intently by his beautiful girl-friend (who does not say a word throughout the scene) he pours out all his Vietnam guilt, obsessions and evasions and ends by giving up all idea of writing. In an interview with me, Resnais characterised this monologue as being in the manner of Jean Cocteau's "Le Bel Indifférent" or "La Voix Humaine" and made it clear that he had conceived it as a deliberately theatrical counterbalance to the more straightforward documentary material provided by most of the other contributors. Thus in a sense this episode of *Loin du Vietnam* is a most vivid illustration of Resnais's concern with the theatre and with actors: Fresson's is the only "inauthentic" face in the whole film, since everyone else, from Fidel Castro down to the most insignificant demonstrator, talks directly from his own experience.

Like Godard (who also uses the device of the monologue), Resnais keeps strictly to a literal interpretation of the title — Far from Vietnam — dealing with the repercussions of the war on European sensibilities. His distrust of the compilation film is clear from the story told by Fresson of the film-shot of a war atrocity that has been used so often that technicians have given it a name, "Gustave", and audiences look out for it as for an old friend. Similarly, Resnais's dislike of direct propaganda leads him to create a non-heroic figure, a perfect example of "bad faith" in the Sartrean sense, torn by an ambivalent attitude to America typical of French intellectuals (cf. Marker's unrealised *L'Amérique Rêve* and Godard's *Made in U.S.A.*) and a man who, like Diego Mora in *La Guerre est finie*, finds the contradictions and complexities of the present situation too much for him. But unlike Diego this character abandons the struggle and as if to emphasise this he is given the same name as the totally nonpolitical hero of *Je t'aime, je t'aime*, Claude Ridder. In *Loin du Vietnam* Resnais thus furnishes a further example of his favourite stylistic device — the effect of an interplay of varying tones and textures — by providing a sketch that is negative and theatrical in a film that is essentially a committed documentary.

At the time of writing, Resnais is at work on the editing of a new feature film, **Je t'aime, je t'aime,** which was shot in Autumn 1967 from a script by Jacques Sternberg, whom Resnais had contacted in 1962 after reading his novel 'Un jour ouvrable'. Like all the director's films since *Marienbad*, *Je t'aime, je t'aime* is the product of a very close collaboration between writer and director spread over a number of years (five in this case). At the beginning Sternberg was left to work alone and he has said that he wrote "fragments of all sorts, the place of which was not fixed in the film. Every possible flashback. Often these insignificant, banal, incomplete scenes did not exceed a page or two. I did ten to thirty a week and I delivered them to Resnais as I wrote them. I worked without any instruction, on my own. The principle was rather that of automatic writing."[68] The writer was encouraged to try out every possible development, but required to provide coherent studies of the main characters. Of Resnais's attitude to these Sternberg has said: "He wants to know everything. But it is not strictly speaking psychology that interests him. It is rather the aura, the tone of the character."[68] When the material amounted to what Sternberg has called "a little mountain of 800 pages" it was Resnais who embarked on the cutting and shaping of it. That he was able to do this with assurance is not surprising since two years before meeting Sternberg he had told an interviewer that he thought methods like automatic writing were indispensable, adding, however, that "there is also the way the material is used, because I think that once automatic writing has given its maximum, you can always choose and do a kind of editing... The idea comes in a purely automatic fashion. Then if I can justify it rationally, I keep it, of course. If, on the other hand, it seems worthless, then I reject it."[5] Sternberg's idea had been "to recount no matter what, without imposing on the spectator any psychological or chronological constraint", and he had envisaged "an elastic film which would last twelve or twenty-four hours. People would have come and gone as they wished, that didn't matter since the story could be taken up at any point."[68] But Resnais, throwing away, as he had done in the case of *Muriel*, enough material to make another film, had reduced this by Summer 1965 to a workable film script without, however, fitting it into the kind of five act pattern he had used in his first four features. After a break while Resnais directed *La Guerre est finie* (on which he had been working simultaneously) the script was revised "sentence by sentence, comma by comma" and the work of shooting it could begin.

While the exact form that *Je t'aime, je t'aime* will take is obviously impossible to ascertain at this stage, the broad outlines that emerge from Sternberg's published accounts and from a conversation with Resnais himself make it clear that the film will be very much a continuation of the earlier features. As if reacting against the idea of repeating himself,

156

however, Resnais has not only abandoned the five act structural pattern that has characterised his work up till now, he has also changed his director of photography (though he plans to work with Sacha Vierny again later) and minimised the use of music. Indeed, at the time when he finished shooting he was unsure whether there would be any musical score at all, though the construction of the film itself will follow the free, 'musical' patterns of, say *Marienbad*. *Je t'aime, je t'aime* marks the end, for the time being, of Resnais's concern with politics and actuality and a return to the investigation of love. Asked what the subject of his new film was, he replied quite simply: "A man meets a woman, that's all." Sternberg's account of the film makes it clear that there is far more to the film than this and reveals how close it is to the "private" sources of Resnais's inspiration and how it carries further the director's investigations into time: "The idea I submitted to Resnais derives from science fiction. It is the story of a time experiment that fails. Scientists project a man into his past and do not succeed in retrieving him. So the film is presented as a series of flashbacks. But when you go back into the past in the cinema, it is almost always to participate in important, privileged scenes. It is as if you were on a psycho-analyst's couch. I wanted on the contrary to choose totally insignificant scenes, *temps morts*. *Je t'aime, je t'aime* is a film in which you can put anything you like. The point of departure is fantastic, what follows, banal and harrowing, like everyday life."[68] As in earlier films, the background setting is important and Sternberg has explained that Brussels was chosen because they "wanted the place to have a sort of neutral character."

This effect is likely to be enhanced by the use of colour which, as in *Muriel*, is employed purely realistically, with no experiments in conveying atmosphere.

Thus over twenty years of film-making Resnais, like all other great directors, has maintained absolute fidelity to his own sources of inspiration and his chosen thematic material. Much has been made of his diversity as a director, the chameleon-like ability to capture the precise tone of another artist's work, to follow a Marguerite Duras film by one of Alain Robbe-Grillet, and to vary each time the angle from which his themes are approached, so that fresh insights are constantly found. Yet it is rather the unity of all his work which is the hallmark of Resnais's greatness: the manner in which he is able to expand his documentary experiments into feature form, mix prose and poetry, realism and fantasy while still remaining true to himself. Above all, he applies a wholly original conception of the film's stylistic potentialities, running largely at variance with current fashion and practice, to a range of subject matter of enormous complexity in its demands for a revolutionary approach to time and narrative structure.

Filmography

The following filmography, based largely on the published researches of Gaston Bounoure and Francis Lacassin, omits Resnais's juvenilia and the 16mm films to which his contribution was purely technical.

A. Films edited by Resnais

Paris 1900 (1947). Directed by Nicole Védrès.

Saint-Tropez, Devoir de Vacances (1952). Directed by Paul Paviot.

La Pointe Courte (1955). Directed by Agnès Varda.

L'Oeil du Maître (1957). Directed by Jacques Doniol-Valcroze.

Broadway by Light (1957). Directed by William Klein.

Paris à l'Automne (1958). Directed by François Reichenbach.

B. Films in 16mm. directed by Resnais

Schéma d'une Identification (1946). Cast. Gérard Philipe and François Chaumette.

Ouvert pour cause d'Inventaire (1946). Also known as *Assieds-toi, veux-tu dans la bergère* or *Affaire classée.* Cast. Danièle Delorme, Nadine Alari, Pierre Trabaud.

Visite à Lucien Coutaud (1947)

Visite à Félix Labisse (1947).

Visite à Hans Hartung (1947).

Visite à César Domela (1947).

Visite à Oscar Dominguez (1947).

Portrait d'Henri Goetz (1947).

La Bague (1947). A mime performed by Marcel Marceau.

Journée Naturelle (1947). In colour. Also known as *Visite à Max Ernst*.

L'Alcool Tue (1947). Produced by Les Films de la Roue. *Direction, photography and editing:* Alain Resnais. *Script:* Remo Forlani and Roland Dubillard. CAST. Roland Dubillard, Remo Forlani and Robert Mendigal *(The workmen);* Claude Charpentier *(The priest);* Christiane Renty and Colette Renty *(The women);* Paul Renty *(The foreman)*.

Les Jardins de Paris (1948). Produced by Les Films de la Roue (Christiane and Paul Renty). *Direction, photography and editing:* Alain Resnais. *Script:* Roland Dubillard.

Châteaux de France (1948). In colour. Produced by Ciné Gimm. *Direction, script, photography and editing:* Alain Resnais.

Van Gogh (1948). For Les Amis de l'Art. Remade as Resnais's first 35mm film.

Malfray (1948). *Direction:* Alain Resnais and Gaston Diehl. *Conception:* Gaston Diehl. *Music:* Pierre Barbaud.

C. Short films in 35mm

VAN GOGH. 1948. Produced by Les Films du Panthéon (Pierre Braunberger). *Direction and editing:* Alain Resnais. *Conception and script:* Robert Hessens and Gaston Diehl. *Commentary:* Gaston Diehl (spoken by

*LA GUERRE EST FINIE:
three focal points in the life
of Diego. Top, comradeship –
Diego (Yves Montand) with
Ramon (Jean Bouise). Centre,
the young plotters. Right,
Marianne (Ingrid Thulin).*

Top, Alain Resnais with script-writer Jacques Sternberg. Centre and right, two stills from their new film JE T'AIME, JE T'AIME.

Claude Dauphin). *Photography:* Henri Ferrand. *Music:* Jacques Besse. 20 minutes.

GAUGUIN. 1950. Produced by Les Films du Panthéon (Pierre Braunberger). *Direction and editing:* Alain Resnais. *Conception* and *script:* Gaston Diehl. *Commentary:* extracts from Paul Gauguin's correspondence (spoken by Jean Servais). *Photography:* Henri Ferrand. *Music:* Darius Milhaud. 11 minutes.

GUERNICA. 1950. Produced by Les Films du Panthéon (Pierre Braunberger). *Direction:* Alain Resnais and Robert Hessens. *Conception and script:* Robert Hessens. *Commentary:* Paul Eluard (spoken by Maria Casarès and Jacques Pruvost). *Photography:* Henri Ferrand. *Camera operators:* André Dumaître and William Novik. *Music:* Guy Bernard. *Orchestra direction:* Marc Vaubourgoin. *Editing:* Alain Resnais. *Sound:* Pierre-Louis Calvet. 11 minutes.

LES STATUES MEURENT AUSSI. 1950-53. Produced by Présence Africaine and Tadié Cinéma. *Direction and script:* Alain Resnais and Chris Marker. *Commentary:* Chris Marker (spoken by Jean Negroni). *Photography:* Ghislain Cloquet. *Music:* Guy Bernard. *Editing:* Alain Resnais. 30 minutes.

NUIT ET BROUILLARD. 1955. Produced by Argos Film and Como Film. *Direction:* Alain Resnais. *Commentary:* Jean Cayrol (spoken by Michel Bouquet). *Historical advisers:* André Michel and Olga Wormser. *Photography:* Ghislain Cloquet and Sacha Vierny. *Music:* Hanns Eisler. *Editing:* Henri Colpi and Jasmine

Chasney. 32 minutes. Black and White and Eastman-color.

TOUTE LA MÉMOIRE DU MONDE. 1956. Produced by Films de la Pléïade (Pierre Braunberger). *Direction and editing:* Alain Resnais. *Conception, script and commentary:* Remo Forlani (spoken by Jacques Dumesnil). *Photography:* Ghislain Cloquet. *Music:* Maurice Jarre. *Orchestra direction:* Georges Delerue. 21 minutes. *With the collaboration of:* Gérard Willemetz, Pierre Goupil, Anne Sarraute, Roger Fleytoux, Claude Joudioux, Jean Cayrol, André Goefers, Jean-Charles Lauthe, Chris and Magic Marker, Phil Davis, Robert Rendigal, Giuletta Caputo, Claudine Merlin, Dominique Raoul Duval, Chester Gould, Denise York, Benigne Caceres, Agnès Varda, Monique Le Porrier, Paulette Borker, André Heinrich, Mme. Searle, Marie-Claire Pasquier, François-Régis Bastide, Joseph Rovan.

LE MYSTÈRE DE L'ATELIER QUINZE. 1957. Produced by Les Films Jacqueline Jacoupy. *Direction:* André Heinrich and Alain Resnais. *Script:* Remo Forlani. *Commentary:* Chris Marker (spoken by Jean-Pierre Grenier). *Photography:* Ghislain Cloquet and Sacha Vierny. *Music:* Pierre Barbaud. *Orchestra direction:* Georges Delerue. *Editing:* Anne Sarraute. 18 minutes. *With the collaboration of:* Chris Marker, Yves Peneau, Jean Brugot, Fernand Marzelle, Claude Joudioux, André Schlotter, Fearless Fosdick, Elisabeth Seibel.

LE CHANT DU STYRÈNE. 1958. Produced by Pierre Braunberger. *Direction and editing:* Alain Resnais.

Commentary: Raymond Queneau (spoken by Pierre Dux). *Photography:* Sacha Vierny. *Music:* Pierre Barbaud. *Orchestra direction:* Georges Delerue. 14 minutes. Eastmancolor.

D. Feature films

HIROSHIMA MON AMOUR. 1959. Produced by Argos Films/Como Films/Daiei Motion Pictures/Pathé Overseas (Samy Halfon). *Direction:* Alain Resnais. *Script and dialogue:* Marguerite Duras. *Photography:* Sacha Vierny (France) and Michio Takahashi (Japan). *Cameramen:* Goupil, Watanabe, Ioda. *Design:* Esaka, Mayo, Petri. *Music:* Giovanni Fusco, Georges Delerue and Japanese music. *Sound:* P. Calvet, Yamamoto, R. Renault. *Editing:* Henri Colpi, Jasmine Chasney, Anne Sarraute. 91 minutes.
CAST. Emmanuelle Riva *(Elle);* Eiji Okada *(Lui);* Bernard Fresson *(L'Allemand);* Stella Dassas *(La Mère);* Pierre Barbaud *(Le Père).*
Shot in 1958. Japanese exteriors at Hiroshima and interiors at Tokyo. French exteriors at Nevers and interiors at Paris studios.

L'ANNÉE DERNIÈRE À MARIENBAD. 1961. Produced by Terra Film/Société Nouvelle des Films Comoran/Précitel/Como Films/Argos Films/Les Films Tamara/Cinétel/Silver Films/Cineriz (Rome). (Pierre Courau and Raymond Froment). *Direction:* Alain Resnais. *Script and dialogue:* Alain Robbe-Grillet. *Photography:* Sacha

Vierny. *Cameraman:* Philippe Brun. *Design:* Jacques Saulnier. *Costumes:* Bernard Evein. *Music:* Francis Seyrig. *Sound:* Guy Villette. *Editing:* Henri Colpi and Jasmine Chasney. 93 minutes.

CAST. Delphine Seyrig *(A);* Giorgio Albertazzi *(X);* Sacha Pitoëff *(M);* and Pierre Barbaud, Françoise Bertin, Luce Garcia-Ville, Héléna Kornel, Jean Lanier, Gérard Lorin, Davide Montemuri, Gilles Quéant, Françoise Spira, Karin Toeche-Mittlet, Wilhelm von Deek, Gabriel Werner.

Shot in 1961. Exteriors at Munich (castles of Nymphenburg, Schleissheim, Amalienburg). Interiors at Photosonor Studios in Paris.

MURIEL OU LE TEMPS D'UN RETOUR. 1963. Produced by Argos Films/Alpha Productions/Eclair/Les Films de la Pléïade/Dear Films (Rome). (Anatole Dauman). *Direction:* Alain Resnais. *Script and dialogue:* Jean Cayrol. *Photography:* Sacha Vierny. *Cameraman:* Philippe Brun. *Design:* Jacques Saulnier. *Music:* Hans Werner Henze (sung by Rita Streich). *Sound:* Antoine Bonfanti. *Editing:* Kenout Peltier and Eric Pluet. 115 minutes.

CAST. Delphine Seyrig *(Hélène);* Jean-Pierre Kerien *(Alphonse);* Nita Klein *(Françoise);* Jean-Baptiste Thierée *(Bernard);* Laurence Badie *(Claudie);* Martine Vatel *(Marie-Do);* Jean Champion *(Ernest);* Claude Sainval *(De Smoke);* Jean Dasté *(l'homme à la chèvre)* and: Martine Vatel, Julien Verdier, Philippe Laudenbach,

Nelly Borgeaud, Catherine de Seynes, Gaston Joly, Gérard Lorin, Wanda Kerien, Jean-Jacques Lagarde, Paul Chevallier, Laure Poillette, Robert Bordenave, Eliane Chevet, Yves Vincent.
Shot in 1962-63. Exteriors in Bologne. Interiors in Paris.

LA GUERRE EST FINIE. 1966. Produced by Sofracima (Paris)/Europa Film (Stockholm) (Alain Quefféléan). *Direction:* Alain Resnais. *Script, dialogue and narration:* Jorge Semprun. *Photography:* Sacha Vierny. *Design:* Jacques Saulnier. *Music:* Giovanni Fusco. *Sound:* Antoine Bonfanti. *Editing:* Eric Pluet. 122 minutes.
CAST. Yves Montand *(Diego)*; Ingrid Thulin *(Marianne)*; Geneviève Bujold *(Nadine)*; Dominique Rozan *(Jude)*; Françoise Bertin *(Carmen)*; Michel Piccoli *(Customs Officer)*; Paul Crauchet *(Roberto)*; Gérard Séty *(Bill)*; Jean Bouise *(Ramon)*; Anouk Ferjac *(Mme. Jude)*; Yvette Etiévant *(Yvette)*; Jean Dasté *(The Chief)*; Annie Farge *(Agnès)*; Gérard Lartigau *(Student leader)*; Jacques Rispal *(Manolo)*; Jean-François Rémi *(Juan)*; Pierre Leproux *(Maker of forged papers)*; Marie Mergey *(Mme. Lopez)*; Marcel Cuvelier *(Chardin)*; Roland Monod *(Antoine)*; Bernard Fresson *(Sarlat)*; Laurence Badie *(Bernadette Pluvier)*; Jose-Maria Flotats *(Miguel)*; Catherine de Seynes *(Janine)*; Claire Duhamel *(Traveller)*; R.-J. Chauffard *(Tramp)*; Jean Larroquette *(Student)*; Martine Vatel *(Student)*; Roger Pelletier *(Inspector)*; Antoine Bourseiller *(Traveller)*; Antoine Vitez *(Air France Employee)*; Jacques Robnard

165

(Pierrot); Paillette *(Old Woman);* Jean Bolo, Pierre Decazes, Jacques Wallet, Pierre Barbaud.
Shot in 1965. Exteriors in France. Interiors in Stockholm.

LOIN DU VIETNAM. 1967. Produced by Slon. *Direction:* Alain Resnais, William Klein, Joris Ivens, Agnès Varda, Claude Lelouch, Jean-Luc Godard. 120 minutes (approx.). *With the collaboration of:* Michèle Ray, Roger Pic, K. S. Karol, Marceline Loridan, François Maspero, Chris Marker, Jacques Sternberg, Jean Lacoutre, Willy Kurant, Jean Boffety, Kien Tham, Denis Clairval, Ghislain Cloquet, Bernard Zitzerman, Alain Levent, Theo Robichet, Antoine Bonfanti, Harold Maury, Claire Grunstein, Alain Frauchet, Didier Beaudet, Florence Malraux, Marie-Louise Guinet, Roger de Menestrol, Ragnar, Jean Ravel, Colette Leloup, Eric Pluet, Albert Jurgensen, Ethel Blum, Michèle Bouder, Christian Quinson, Jean Larivière, Maurice Garrel, Bernard Fresson, Karen Blanguernon, Anne Bellec, Valérie Mayoux.

JE T'AIME, JE T'AIME. 1968. Produced by Parc Film — Mag Bodard. *Direction:* Alain Resnais. *Script and dialogue:* Jacques Sternberg. *Photography:* Jean Boffety. *Design:* Jacques Dugied. *Sound:* Antoine Bonfanti.
CAST. Claude Rich *(Claude Ridder)*, Olga Georges-Picot *(Catrine)*, Anouk Ferjac *(Winna)*, Marie-Blanche Vergne *(Young woman in the tram)* and Carla Marlier, Alain McMoy, Yves Kerboul, Vania Vilers, Van Doude,

166

Dominique Rozan.

Shot in Autumn 1967 (September to November). Exteriors in Brussels and France. Interiors in Paris.

E. Unrealised Projects

Pierrot Mon Ami (1951). From the novel by Raymond Queneau.

Les Mauvais Coups (1951). From the novel by Roger Vailland.

Un Dimanche tous ensemble (1956). Scripted by Remo Forlani.

L'Ile Noire (1957). Scripted by Remo Forlani, from one of Hergé's adventures of Tintin.

La Tête contre les Murs (1957). From the novel by Hervé Bazin.

Fantômas

Red Ryder

L'Affaire Dreyfus

Vie de Louis Feuillade

Vie de Napoléon

La Permission (1960). From the novel by Daniel Anselme.

A Suivre, à n'en plus finir (1960). Scripted by Anne-Marie de Villaine.

Les Aventures d'Harry Dickson. Scripted by Frédéric de Towarnicki.

Bibliography

The most accessible sources of comments by Resnais and his collaborators are *Premier Plan* 18 (which reprints in full Nos. 2-9 below), Gaston Bounoure's monograph (containing No. 1, Nos. 42-48 and many extracts), the *Spécial Resnais* issue of *L'Avant-Scène du Cinéma* 61-2 (quoting comments by Resnais, his scriptwriters and reviewers, including Nos. 61-4 below), and the special number of *L'Arc* 31 (which prints Nos. 65-78). The number beside each entry is the one used in the text to indicate the source of quotations.

A. Interviews and Statements by Resnais alone

1.   Alain Resnais: "Une Expérience" in *Ciné-Club* No. 3 (Dec. 1948)
2.   —, in *Premier Plan* (dated 1956)
3.   —with Gilbert Guez, in *Cinémonde* (14 Mar. 1961)
4.   —with Sylvain Roumette, in *Clarté* No. 33 (Feb. 1961)
5.   —with Jean Carta & Michel Mesnil, in *Esprit* No. 6 (June 1960)
6.   —with Michel Delahaye, in *Cinéma 59* No. 38 (July 1959)
7.   —with Max Egly, in *Image et Son* No. 128 (Feb. 1960)
8.   —with Yvonne Baby, in *Le Monde* (29 Aug. 1961)
9.   —with André S. Labarthe & Jacques Rivette, in *Cahiers du Cinéma* No. 123 (Sept. 1961). Translated by Raymond Durgnat in *Films and Filming* (Feb. 1962) and by Rose Kaplan in *New York Film Bulletin* Vol. 3, No. 2
10. —with François Truffaut, in *Arts* (20 Feb. 1956)
11. —with Yvonne Baby, in *Lettres Françaises* No. 118 (Apr. 1957)

168

12. —with Anne Philippe, in *Lettres Françaises* (12-18 Mar. 1959)
13. —, in *Lettres Françaises* (14-20 May 1959)
14. —with Noel Burch, in *Film Quarterly* (Spring 1960)
15. —with Georges Hilleret, in *Sept Jours* (11 Aug. 1960)
16. —with Nicole Zand, in *France Observateur* (18 May 1961)
17. —with Hubert Juin, in *Lettres Françaises* (10-18 Aug. 1961)
18. —with Bernard Giquel, in *Paris Match*
19. —with Pierre Wildenstein, in *Téléciné* No. 88
20. —with Pierre Uytterhoeven, in *Image et Son* No. 148 (Feb. 1962)
21. —, in 'Tu n'as rien vu à Hiroshima' (ed. Raymond Ravar. Université Libre de Bruxelles. 1962)
22. —, in *Télérama* (Dec. 19, 1962)
23. —, in *Téléciné* 118
24. — with Guy Allombert, in *La Cinématographie Française* (Dec. 22, 1962)
25. —, in *Cino Cubano* No. 5 (1962, in Spanish)
26. —, in *Film Ideal* (Mar. 15, 1963, in Spanish)
27. —with Robert Benayoun, in *Positif* Nos. 50-2 (Mar. 1963)
28. —with Alain Le Bris & Michel Caen, in *La Cinématographie Française* (Aug.-Sept. 1964)
29. Alain Resnais: 'Il a porté mes rêves à l'écran' in Francis Lacassin's monograph 'Louis Feuillade' (Editions Seghers. Paris. 1964)
30. —with Marcel Martin, in *Cinéma 65* Nos. 91-92 (Dec.

1964-Jan. 1965). Reprinted in German in Ulrich Gregor: 'Wie Sie Filmen' — Sigbert Mohn Verlag. Gutersloh. 1966.

31. —, in *Cinéma 66* No. 106 (May 1966)
32. —with Yvonne Baby in *Le Monde* (May 11, 1966)
33. —, in *Cinéma 66* No. 109 (Sept.-Oct. 1966)
34. Alain Resnais: statement on censorship, in *Jeune Cinéma* 16 (June-July 1966)
35. —with Guy Gauthier, in *Image et Son* No. 196 (July 1966)
36. —, in *Positif* (Oct. 1966)
37. —with Adrian Maben, in *Films and Filming* (Oct. 1966)
38. —with Bernard Pingaud, in *L'Arc* No. 31 (1967)

B. Joint Interviews and Statements

39. Resnais and Alain Robbe-Grillet, with Pierre Billard, in *Cinéma 61* No. 61 (Nov.-Dec. 1961)
40. Resnais and Alain Robbe-Grillet, with André S. Labarthe and Jacques Rivette, in *Cahiers du Cinéma* No. 123 (Sept. 1961). Translated by Raymond Durgnat in *Films and Filming* (Mar. 1962) and by Rose Kaplan in *New York Film Bulletin* Vol. 3 No. 2.
41. Resnais and Jean Cayrol, with Pierre Billard in *Cinéma 63* No. 80 (Nov. 1963). Largely reprinted in preface to published script of *Muriel*.

C. Statements by Friends and Collaborators

42. Jean Cayrol: 'Nuit et Brouillard' (Bounoure).
43. Georges et Maurice Hilleret: 'Dans un bureau, rue

Pierre-Charron' *(ibid)*

44. André Voisin: 'Sous les néons de l'Escurial' *(ibid)*
45. Danièle Delorme: 'Au Théâtre de l'Oeuvre' *(ibid)*
46. Agnès Varda: 'Dans une chambre haute' *(ibid)*
47. Emmanuelle Riva: 'Au Café des Deux Magots' *(ibid)*
48. Sacha Vierny: 'Devant ma table de travail' *(ibid)*
49. Henri Colpi: 'Musique d'*Hiroshima*' in *Cahiers du Cinéma* No. 103 Jan. 1960. Reprinted in 'Défense et Illustration de la Musique dans le Film' (Serdoc. Lyon. 1963)
50. Henri Colpi: 'Editing *Hiroshima mon Amour*' in *Sight and Sound* Vol. 29 No. 1. (Winter 1960-1)
51. Henri Colpi: interview in *New York Film Bulletin*. Vol. 3 No. 2
52. Marguerite Duras: interview in *Cinéma 59* No. 38 (July 1959)
53. Marguerite Duras: interview in *Image et Son* No. 128 (Feb. 1960. Partly reprinted in preface to the *L'Avant-Scène* script.
54. Marguerite Duras: interview with Richard Roud, in *Sight and Sound* Vol. 29 No. 1 (Winter 1960-1)
55. Alain Robbe-Grillet: interview with Gordon Reid in *Continental Film Review*
56. Jean Cayrol: interview with Luce Sand, in *Jeune Cinéma* 20 (Feb. 1967)
57. Jean Cayrol: statement in publicity material distributed by United Artists
58. Jean Cayrol: in *Télérama* (20 Sept. 1964)
59. Jorge Semprun: statement in *Arts*. Reprinted in

171

publicity material

60. Jorge Semprun: interview with Andrée Tournès in *Jeune Cinéma* 16 (June-July 1966)

61. Remo Forlani: 'L'Alcool tue' *(L'Avant-Scène* 61-2)

62. André Heinrich: 'Le Mystère de l'Atelier Quinze' *(ibid)*

63. Francis Lacassin: 'Les films "amicaux" inconnus' *(ibid)*

64. Francis Lacassin: 'Alain Resnais et les bandes dessinées' *(ibid)*. Translated as 'Dick Tracy meets Muriel' in *Sight and Sound* Vol. 36 No. 2 (Spring 1967)

65. Jean Cayrol on the writing of *Muriel (L'Arc* No. 31)

66. Jorge Semprun on the writing of *La Guerre est finie (ibid)*

67. Frédéric de Towarnicki on the writing of *Les Aventures d'Harry Dickson (ibid)*

68. Jacques Sternberg on the writing of *Je t'aime, je t'aime (ibid)*

69. Alain Quefféléan on producing a Resnais film *(ibid)*

70. Sylvette Baudrot on her work as continuity girl *(ibid)*

71. Jacques Saulnier on designing for Resnais *(ibid)*

72. Ghislain Cloquet on photographing Resnais's shorts *(ibid)*

73. Philippe Brun on his work as cameraman *(ibid)*

74. Delphine Seyrig on acting for Resnais *(ibid)*

75. Jean Dasté on Resnais and actors *(ibid)*

76. Eric Pluet on editing for Resnais *(ibid)*

77. Francis Seyrig on the music for *Marienbad (ibid)*

78. Pierre Barbaud on Resnais and music *(ibid)*

Two volumes of essays are also important:

79. Jean Cayrol and Claude Durand: 'Le Droit de Regard'

(Editions du Seuil. Paris. 1963)

80. Alain Robbe-Grillet: 'Pour un nouveau roman' (Editions de Minuit. Paris. 1963). Translated in 'Snapshots and Towards a New Novel' (John Calder. London.1965)

D. Published Scripts and Commentaries

81. 'Van Gogh' in *L'Avant-Scène du Cinéma* No. 61-2 ('Spécial Resnais') (July-Sept. 1966)

82. 'Guernica' in *L'Avant-Scène du Cinéma* No. 38 (June 1964)

83. 'Les Statues meurent aussi' in Chris Marker: 'Commentaires' (Editions du Seuil. Paris. 1961)

84. 'Nuit et Brouillard' (commentary only) in *L'Avant-Scène du Cinéma* No. 1 (Feb. 1961)

85. 'Toute la mémoire du monde' in *L'Avant-Scène du Cinéma* No. 52 (Oct. 1965)

86. 'Le Mystère de l'Atelier Quinze' in *L'Avant-Scène du Cinéma* No. 61-2 (July-Sept. 1966)

87. 'Le Chant du Styrène' (commentary only) in *L'Avant-Scène du Cinéma* No. 1 (Feb. 1961)

88. 'Hiroshima mon Amour' — Marguerite Duras's script (with her notes): Gallimard. Paris. 1960. Translated into German in 'Spektakulum: Texte moderner Filme' — Suhrkamp Verlag. Frankfurt. 1961. Translated into English: Calder and Boyars. London. 1966.

89. 'Hiroshima mon Amour' — Resnais's shooting script in *L'Avant-Scène du Cinéma* No. 61-2 ('Spécial Resnais') (July-Sept. 1966)

90. 'L'Année Dernière à Marienbad' — script with an intro-

duction by Robbe-Grillet: Editions de Minuit. Paris. 1961. Translated into English: John Calder. London. 1961.

91. 'Muriel' — script with notes by Cayrol: Editions du Seuil. Paris. 1963.

92. 'La Guerre est finie' — script: Gallimard. Paris. 1966.

E. Principal Studies of Resnais's Work

93. *Cahiers du Cinéma* No. 96. *(Hiroshima* discussion) July 1959.

94. *Premier Plan* No. 4 (Michel Delahaye and Henri Colpi). Serdoc. Lyon. 1959.

95. André Bazin in 'Qu'est-ce que le Cinéma' Vol II. Edition du Cerf. Paris. 1959.

96. *Premier Plan* No. 18 (Bernard Pingaud). Serdoc. Lyon. 1961.

97. Gaston Bounoure: 'Alain Resnais'. Cinéma d'Aujourd-hui No. 5. Editions Seghers. Paris. 1962.

98. Raymond Ravar (ed.): 'Tu n'as rien vu à Hiroshima'. Université Libre de Bruxelles. 1962.

99. Peter Cowie in 'Antonioni-Bergman-Resnais'. Tantivy Press. London. 1963.

100. *Art Sept* No.1: 'Un Cinéma Réel'. Jan-Mar. 1963.

101. *Cahiers du Cinéma* No. 159 (*Muriel* discussion) Nov. 1963.

102. John Russell Taylor in 'Cinema Eye, Cinema Ear'. Methuen. London. 1964.

103. Eric Rhode in 'Tower of Babel'. Weidenfeld and Nicolson. London. 1966.

104. *L'Avant-Scène du Cinéma* No. 61-2: 'Spécial Resnais'. July-Sept. 1966.
105. *Cahiers du Cinéma* No. 185: 'Film et Roman: Problèmes du Récit'. Dec. 1966.
106. *L'Arc* No. 31 (ed. Bernard Pingaud). 1967.
107. *Image et Son* No. 210 (Nov. 1967). 'Un Cinéma Politique: L'œuvre de Resnais' by René Prédal.